KILLER SOCIALS

The **Killer** Social Media Strategy
for Entrepreneurial Success

By Maria-Teresa Andreacchi

You don't need 100,000 followers to generate six figures
from social media. You just need a **killer** strategy.

For permission requests, contact the author at:
info@soarmediagroupinc.com
www.soarmediagroupinc.com

First Edition: February, 2025

ISBN: 978-1-0689338-1-3

To those who inspired me to put pen to paper.

CONTENTS

Letter from the Author

Have you ever heard of the lyrics 'started from the bottom now we're here'? I don't think Drake was referencing social media, but his words perfectly describe where it can take you.

By now, you've probably heard of overnight success stories that took off from social media. It's a platform where small businesses can compete with big brands, making it especially attractive to entrepreneurs without multi-million dollar budgets.

However, figuring out where to start can feel like standing at the base of Mount Everest. It's overwhelming at best.

Social media managers need to be storytellers, strategists, photographers, videographers, community managers, content creators, planners, and networkers. Their roles are ever-changing. They need to be masters at multitasking and able to adapt to new platform changes in an instant.

The job goes beyond deciding what to post, on which social network, and at what time. Instead, social media managers are in a constant battle of strategy and entertainment. Every day they are finding the balance between sharing an authentic message and capturing attention.

In 2021 Sprout Social reported that 55% of consumers learn about brands through social media, a figure that jumps to 78% for Generation Z and 61% for Millennials. Social media is no longer a nice-to-have. It's a necessity. Because of this, it is essential for entrepreneurs to understand how social media works.

Whether you are new to social media or looking to join additional social networks, this book will show you the processes, best practices, strategy, and tips you need to succeed. If you want to kill it on social media, you need a killer strategy. And my formula is a proven way to see success online.

As you read through this book, I want you to keep one thing in mind: social media will give you as much as you put into it.

Your story, your brand, your product — it is as deserving of an online audience as any other, but you need to be willing to give it your all.

Now that you're standing at the base of the mountain, are you ready to climb?

— Maria-Teresa Andreacchi,
Owner and Lead Strategist of Soar Media Group Inc.
Instagram: @mariateresa_andreacchi

Social media is a rapidly changing landscape. Though the tips in this book are evergreen, I recommend following @soarmediagroupinc on Instagram so you can stay up-to-date with the newest social media trends.

CHAPTER 1

How I Turned Social Media into a Career

At 27, I said goodbye to the comfort of a full-time job and started my journey as a business owner. I had absolutely no business experience and I didn't come from a family of entrepreneurs. Despite this, I still managed to create something unique: a remote social media agency that helps brands stand out through content marketing. I saw an opportunity to disrupt traditional marketing and PR agencies in Toronto and I took it.

Drawing from my experiences as a lifestyle blogger and travel writer, I focused on storytelling, visual aesthetics, and assembling a talented team. I spent twelve hours a day building my business and I used social media to do it.

Over the past few years, I've been through the ups and downs of running a business, learning to think differently and see failure as a part of the process.

The biggest thing I've learned? To kill it in life, you've got to play to your strengths, even if other people might see them as weaknesses.

When I finished university I felt defeated. Not only did I have little job prospects, but I had a very hard time fitting in. In fact, the day of my commencement, the Teacher's College Department Head at Brock University snickered before I went on stage, and said, "I'm surprised YOU graduated with honours."

My crime? I was live-tweeting takeaways during class. Twitter was still new and few people knew what it was. From her perspective, I was playing on my phone during class and that was a big no.

Perhaps I could have been like the other girls. I could have stopped using Twitter as my SparkNotes. Or I could have deactivated my account. But I didn't. I was doing something different. And that was my curse.

During university, I volunteered at every teaching conference to get ahead. But unfortunately, these efforts yielded absolutely no networking opportunities. To top it all off, our professors would frequently remind us of the grim job market. The teaching industry had too many graduates and too few jobs.

It was disheartening, and I started to feel like my years of education were all for nothing.

I had spent five years learning, volunteering, and excelling only to have my last year of university nearly break me.

A few months after commencement a friend told me she applied for teaching jobs in the UK and everything suddenly clicked. This was what I needed. I needed a fresh start.

I was hired after my second interview so I packed up my life and moved across the Atlantic. In one week, I became Miss. A to a Year 4 class in England.

Looking back, that move of independence — moving across the world, living on my own, working in a new country — helped me grow in a way that staying home never would have. It was what inspired my digital journey and led me to where I am now. Because it was here, in England, that I started to take my social media and digital identity seriously.

At first, I thought incorporating technology into my classroom would satiate my digital craving. Earlier in my practicum, I made a blog for the students and linked their homework via Google Drive.

"There's no excuse that you didn't bring your homework home!" I would say.

And it worked. The entire class excelled.

Then in England, I'd include YouTube videos in my lessons and let the students use Google whenever they needed support. I even connected with a Head Teacher on Twitter who gave me mentorship and advice.

But I quickly realized through this process that teaching wasn't my passion. The students loved me and I loved them. Yet, my heart wasn't in it. I wanted more digital experiences.

"To kill it in life, you've got to play to your strengths, even if other people might see them as weaknesses."

One rainy night in England, my best friend asked me over FaceTime, "What are you doing?"

"What do you mean?" I replied.

"You've never wanted to teach. You hate it. Your parents told you what to do and you did it. When are you going to go after what you really want?"

She was right and I knew it.

That night I started a blog called Fashion.Food.Flair. A tacky name, but a leap of faith into a new career. On the 'about me' page I wrote: This blog is to update my friends and family back home. I hope you love my cooking, travel visits, and fashion finds as much as I do!

That same month I applied to Centennial College in Toronto for a PR & Communications postgraduate degree. And a few months later I was on a flight back home, leaving my teaching career in the clouds.

Little did I know, this move would lay the groundwork for my future success. I was hired as part of the social media team at Meridian Credit Union right out of Centennial College.

I was juggling full-time work and nocturnal blogging sessions, but my dedication started to pay off. I was picked up by a PR agency as a 'blogger' and within the blink of an eye, I was being invited to every exclusive media event in Toronto.

My days were spent working full-time, my nights were spent blogging, and my weekends were spent creating content. I couldn't stop. I felt like I had found my purpose.

I learned what SEO was and how to make my content appear on the first page of Google. I taught myself how to take photos and edit videos. I started to use social media to connect with people and share my content. I wasn't getting paid, but I was okay with that because I loved what I was doing.

All I could think was about: content, content, content.

Next came travel writing — a freelance job I took on while working full-time. I had reached out to a travel editor I met at a food blogging event, took her for coffee and said:

"Are there any chances to write a small piece? Even if it's only 100 words. I don't mind writing for free. If you like it, you can pay for it. If you don't like it, no worries."

It turned out that the magazine did like my writing (even though I had no prior professional writing experience). That

" For the first time ever, the playing field is level. Startups have the same opportunity to thrive as big-name brands."

100-word piece turned into a regular contribution, and pretty soon I was in charge of an entire column called the Packing List. A year later I went to Cinque Terre, Italy on a personal trip. Knowing the magazine had a European edition coming up, I reached out again.

"Can I write an article about Cinque Terre? No commitments. I'll write it for free and if you don't like it, I'll post it on my blog. But if you do like it, you can buy the story."

Again, they liked it.

During the time I was travel writing, I had also changed jobs. I left Meridian Credit Union to go to a small PR agency. I wanted more creative freedom in my job and needed a change of pace. Conveniently enough, Meridian reached out a year later and asked me to work freelance for them.

My life had become beautifully and intentionally chaotic. While working full-time at the agency, I was also travel writing, blogging, and creating social media campaigns for Canada's largest credit union.

A few months after my Cinque Terre article was published, I was asked to go on a press trip to Taiwan to write about solo travel as a woman. It was here, on a dewy morning in Sun Moon Lake, that I realized perseverance equals success; that challenges are paramount to growth; that being different is a blessing.

I wasn't the misunderstood girl in teacher's college any more. I was someone who could pack up and move abroad.

I could change careers. I could make money from social media. I could travel alone to the other end of the world and be perfectly okay. The world was my oyster.

Now that's not to say that Soar Media Group suddenly started out of nowhere. I made a commitment that I wouldn't leave my full-time job until my freelance income matched my full-time income. My move to go out on my own was a calculated risk. But that didn't make it any less scary.

The week after I came back from Taiwan, I gave my two weeks notice, registered Soar Media Group as a business and went full force.

Despite a modest social media following (only 5,000 Instagram followers at the time), I used content marketing to build Soar Media Group into a six-figure business.

My strategy was simple. I used the **KILLER** framework, a strategy that I'm only now sharing in this book. It's how someone like me, with no prior business experience, was able to grow and sustain a social media agency that has financially supported me and my family since 2017.

Killer Socials is more than just a book — it's a roadmap to your potential, a testament to the power of vision, and a tribute to the indomitable spirit of the entrepreneurial mind.

Why Social Media is Crucial for Entrepreneurial Success

Social media isn't just a marketing tool, it's an engine driving modern business growth. Countless success stories have shown the impact of social media on entrepreneurial ventures. New entrepreneurs and influencers are regularly seen building lucrative businesses straight from an Instagram feed. In months they are able to establish credibility, and cultivate a loyal customer base. Two things that used to require millions of dollars in marketing.

For the first time ever, the playing field is level. Startups have the same opportunity to thrive as big-name brands.

Why? Because consumers now live online. They discover new products, research brands, and make purchasing decisions all through social media. If your business isn't there, you're missing out—simple as that.

Unlike traditional advertising, social media allows businesses to reach and engage with a global audience. By maintaining an active social media presence, businesses can stay up to date with evolving consumer behaviours, adapt marketing strategies accordingly, and remain competitive in an ever changing marketplace.

More importantly, social media puts you face-to-face with your audience—no call centres, no gatekeepers. It's instant feedback, real connections, and insight into your customers' lives that inform smarter business decisions.

Compared to traditional advertising methods, social media marketing is also more cost-effective. Even the smallest marketing budgets are allowed. Whether you've got $100 or $10,000, you can run targeted ads, reach niche audiences, and make your budget work harder than any TV spot or billboard ever could.

My message is this: social media is a non-negotiable for entrepreneurs. It keeps you relevant, puts you in the game with the big players, and builds a community that will take your business places you never thought possible.

Chapter Summary

- Social media is a powerful tool to build a career, even with a modest following.
- Lean into your unique strengths, even if others misinterpret them. Doing things differently (like live-tweeting during lessons) can eventually become your advantage.
- Building a social media business doesn't require experience; it requires the willingness to learn, adapt, and embrace failure as a stepping stone to growth.
- Connecting with people, creating content consistently, and offering value — even for free initially — opens doors and leads to opportunities that build credibility and income.

CHAPTER 2

Social Media's Allure & Managerial Pitfalls

Social media businesses exchange their services for attention, and from that attention they gather data. Their primary objective is to keep you on their platforms for as long as possible. The more you use social media, the more the social media companies profit from advertisers. And the more your content retains attention, the more you're likely to get pushed to new users. This is why understanding the psychology behind social media is so important.

Why is Social Media so Alluring?

Dopamine Highs

Social media uses positive feedback (likes and comments) to trigger dopamine receptors. By activating our reward systems, these platforms hold our attention.

As a brand, you can use this to your advantage by engaging with your audience. Follow your customers, like their posts, and comment on their life events. This will give them a dopamine kick and make you memorable. It's a classic case: people don't remember what you say, they remember how you made them feel. Engaging positively with your followers like this keeps you top of mind.

Fear of Missing Out (FOMO)

Have you ever heard of the phrase "Instagram made me do it"? FOMO occurs when others feel anxious about missing out on what those around them are using, buying, or experiencing. This fear often drives purchase decisions and increased usage.

As a former travel writer I found FOMO was especially strong within the travel community, often resulting in overtourism at certain destinations. In fact, at one point in my writing career I had to change my *Instagram Worthy Destinations* story to *Instagram Worthy Destinations You Didn't Know About* so that we could highlight locations travellers could enjoy without overcrowding.

We also see this when brands are able to create a limited edition 'it' product. If marketed to the correct audience using the right influencers, a product can trigger FOMO, resulting in an explosion of sales.

Think Kylie Jenner in the late 2010s with her one-time collections and limited-quantity lip kits. People had so much FOMO that it wasn't long before counterfeit Kylie Cosmetics started to hit the streets.

FOMO can be a bad thing for users who fall into its trap, but good for brands looking to capitalize on psychological marketing.

Launching limited edition products, limited-space events, or selecting carefully curated influencers for a launch are all an integral part of building FOMO.

Belonging and Connection

Social media is a place for people to connect with friends, family, and colleagues, as well as discover niche communities. There is a basic human need for social interaction and connection, and social media taps right into this. This was especially prominent during the COVID-19 pandemic when social media usage skyrocketed.

Communities on social media

- Interest-based communities
- Professional communities
- Fandom communities
- Support groups
- Social causes and activism communities
- Geographical communities
- Niche communities
- Online learning communities
- Influencer communities
- Entrepreneurial communities
- Parenting communities
- Health and wellness communities

According to the University of Connecticut, over 70% of people reported increased usage of social media at this time.

This belonging is why it's so important to build an authentic community on social media. Social media should never be about you. Instead, it should be about what you offer other people. Why should they follow you? What value do you bring to the table? How do you make them feel connected? How are you part of their community?

"Social media should never be about you. Instead, it should be about what you offer other people."

News Updates

Updates, trends, and news have never travelled as fast as they do now. And since COVID-19, the number of social media news creators has exploded. Think Joe Rogan (Podcaster), Kim Iversen (YouTuber), or Russell Brand (YouTuber). These unconventional media sources reach millions of users, and for many, have replaced legacy media all together.

According to a study by the Pew Research Center, social media users are more likely to use these platforms to stay informed about news and current events, and to engage in political discourse.

No one is better at using social media to update customers than Taylor Swift. Taylor Swift used social media alone to launch her best-selling Reputation album by sharing updates and Easter eggs from her account. Easter eggs in the context of media and entertainment are hidden messages, clues, or inside jokes embedded within content that fans can discover. They often require keen observation and knowledge of previous works to fully understand and appreciate.

Using social media to share company news or informing customers about relevant events that may impact your business is a smart way to engage your audience.

Self-expression

All walks of life turn to social media to creatively share their authentic selves. Social media breaks down the barriers of geographical or societal confinements. You can be a finance-driven professional who truly loves fitness and just wants to share workout videos, or a busy mom who has a knack for comedy and celebrity impressions.

Whatever it is you need to express, if it's done authentically, there is a community — and likely a following — waiting to cheer you on.

Reviews and Recommendations

Many buyers are also on social media to look for reviews and recommendations. In fact, 27.9% of people use social media to find inspiration for things to do and buy and 23% do so to see what content their favourite brands are posting.

Reviews and recommendations on social media can take various forms, depending on the platform and the preferences of the users. Here are some common examples:

Text Reviews: Text-based reviews highlight experiences with a product, service, or business. These reviews can vary in length and detail, ranging from a brief comment to a comprehensive evaluation.

Photo Reviews: A photo showing a product or service is especially powerful. It takes away the fear of buying the wrong product or wondering, "What does this actually look like? What does this actually do?"

Video Reviews: Video reviews show products or services in action. Video reviews can be particularly engaging and influential on social media.

Why Do Brands Use Social Media?

- To raise brand awareness.
- To build a cult-like following.
- To connect with communities.
- To build relationships with customers.
- To get immediate feedback.
- To rank higher on search engines and build passive traffic.
- To minimize marketing cost without sacrificing quality.
- To build brand loyalty.
- To generate audience insights.
- To gain competitor insights.

Overall, reviews and recommendations on social media build trust and credibility for businesses and influence purchasing decisions for consumers.

This is why it's essential to have a prominent online presence, and to connect with influencers in your niche community. According to Sprout Social, 49% of consumers claim that they depend on influencer recommendations on social media to inform their purchasing decision.

For Entertainment

A few months ago, a client told me that she watches funny YouTube videos before bed with her child. I wasn't surprised. Watching funny Instagram videos with my husband is one of my favourite things to do.

It's not uncommon to see up-and-coming actors, journalists, and experts ditch traditional methods of distribution to instead create their own channels to entertain audiences.

With endless video, text, and imagery, social media has become a highly entertaining digital space. And though I am a firm believer in social media breaks and limited online time for youth, the breadth of entertainment on social media is undoubtedly enjoyable.

Business and Marketing

Social media is a cost-effective way for brands and businesses to reach new audiences and communicate with existing ones. Gone are the days where multi-million dollar budgets are needed to get eyeballs on your product or service.

I've seen local restaurants use Instagram stories to share daily menus, local estheticians use Instagram to find and book new customers, and indie brands use micro-influencers to bring their brand from 0 to thousands. In fact, when planning my wedding, I used Instagram to find and book all my vendors! Nothing shows what you're capable of better than real-time videos, tagged images from customers, or curated photos of your best work.

For Networking

Social media platforms connect users from all around the world, and offer unparalleled opportunities for professional networking. Social circles can be expanded or tapped into to build beneficial relationships for personal and career growth.

Both solopreneurs and brands need to be following leaders in your network. Follow competitor brands, brands in your category, or brands you want to work with.

"Whatever it is you need to express, if it's done authentically, there is a community and likely a following waiting to cheer you on."

When managing a client's social media, we often spend time following key influencers, news editors, and magazine writers. Giving select accounts a follow and liking their content is a good way to softly introduce yourself before fully reaching out — it's social networking 101.

Deadly Social Media Traps

Social media isn't all fun and games. There is a negative side to social media too. Though we could spend hours discussing the downsides, there are two key issues that you need to be aware of: information overload and echo chambers.

Information overload on social media is a real thing, especially when you're spending 4hrs+ a day scrolling and posting. This constant stream of information and stimuli can lead to cognitive overload.

Cognitive overload refers to a condition where the brain's capacity to process and manage incoming information exceeds its available resources. It occurs when individuals are presented with more information than they can effectively process, leading to difficulties in understanding, decision-making, and memory retention. This overload can impair concentration, increase stress levels, and reduce overall cognitive performance.

Decreased productivity, difficulty focusing, and an increased risk of mental fatigue are all signs of information overload and need to be taken seriously. Knowing when to indulge in social media and when to focus is important for long-term success. Long story short: don't doom scroll without a purpose. Ever.

The second most deadly social media trap is echo chambers. Echo chambers occur when social media algorithms show users content that aligns with their existing beliefs and preferences. This can contribute to a lack of social awareness as people may become less exposed to diverse viewpoints and more entrenched in their own beliefs. This occurs when the person running a social media account is viewing or engaging with content that relates to them personally and not the brand.

Your job as a social media manager is to understand who your audience is and the topics that that your audience cares about. Be mindful of treating your brand's social media account as your own. When you're sucked into an echo chamber, it's difficult to see what's really going on in the social space.

"Knowing when to indulge in social media and when to focus is important for long-term success."

Chapter Summary

- Social media platforms have billions of users and billions of opportunities to connect your brand with customers.
- By using social media strategically, businesses can build a strong online presence, engage with their target audience, and drive business growth and success.
- Psychological factors such as dopamine highs from positive feedback, fear of missing out (FOMO), and the need for belonging contribute to social media's allure.
- Social media communities are an integral part of brand growth. Know your community and make yourself known to them.
- Social media serves as a hub for news updates, personal expression, reviews, recommendations, entertainment, business marketing, and networking.
- Don’t fall into deadly social media traps like information overload and echo chambers, which can hinder success for social media managers and users alike. Understanding these dynamics is crucial for navigating the social media landscape effectively.

CHAPTER 3

Picking the Right Social Media Platform

The social media world is constantly changing. By doing your research, and understanding which platform speaks to your audience, you can better reach customers and make social media a strong revenue source.

To see success, you need to be intentional about which platforms are best suited for your brand. The only way to determine your business's best social media platforms is by focusing on where your target audience is.

Factors to consider are:

What resources do you have in-house to support strategy, scheduling, creating content, and community management? Social media is a full-time job so you need to be intentional about where you are going to place your efforts. This is the biggest mistake we see clients making when they decide to bring social media in-house. They underestimate how much time and skill is needed, and then get upset when the account begins to lose followers.

If bringing this in-house, what platform are you most confident using? Think about your skills and what medium you can best use for storytelling and providing value. For example, choosing a video-based platform if you're not confident being in front of the camera isn't playing to your strengths.

What do you hope to achieve from using social media? Having a clear objective, such as "selling my product", will help you better identify the platform that is used by your audience.

A Breakdown of the Major Social Media Platforms and Their Demographics

TikTok

If you somehow missed the explosion of TikTok in 2020, it's a short video-sharing platform that blends music with stickers, text, and video clips. Since its inception in 2016, TikTok has become one of the key platforms in the social media industry. TikTok's main demographic is millennials (25 to 40-year-olds) and Gen Z (12 to 27-year-olds) which make up 62% of the app's audience. TikTok is, by far, the hottest social media platform right now and it keeps getting bigger with new trends developing everyday.

If your business doesn't have the resources or time to develop YouTube videos, TikTok is a great starting point. Since all videos are created in-app, TikTok provides tools and features that allow users with no editing experience to create videos with ease.

Instead of focusing on the duration of your video for TikTok, it's important to focus on what value you are offering. Whether it takes you 15 seconds to offer valuable advice, or 60 seconds, it doesn't matter. Be realistic with yourself and use the data metrics to guide your content. If people are dropping off after 2 seconds, or your video is being viewed by less than 1,000 people, it's because it's not good. When you change your content strategy to focus on giving value to your audience, you will see an uptick in views.

We will talk about how to offer value in later chapters but here is a good cheat sheet:

- Offer tips or tricks. Be concise with these tips and don't drag on.
- Share a story that inspires others.
- Entertain your audience with humour.
- Never share something that has absolutely no value for your audience.

Why use TikTok? TikTok specializes in short, engaging video content, ideal for capturing attention quickly. TikTok stands out from YouTube Shorts and Instagram Reels by fostering a unique, algorithm-driven discovery experience that propels content from ordinary users into viral sensations, creating a dynamic platform for creativity and engagement.

Instagram

Instagram has billions of monthly users and is growing exponentially as time progresses. The platform is primarily used by millennials and Gen Z, so if that is your target audience then Instagram is where you need to be. That said, we are slowly seeing the 45+ demographic begin to join so it's likely that Instagram — from a long-term investment strategy — is a good platform for virtually any brand to use.

Instagram has also integrated e-commerce into their platform so users can purchase products directly from a post. According to Hootsuite, 130 million Instagram users tap on shopping-based posts every month, which is a huge factor if you are selling products online.

Why use Instagram? Instagram is highly visual, making it ideal for showcasing products, lifestyle, and brand aesthetics.

Did you know?

Over 130 million Instagram users tap on in-app shopping features every month.

Facebook

Facebook is a classic, and easy-to-pick-up platform that is accessible for all ages. In fact, seniors are the fastest-growing demographic on Facebook in the US. Although Facebook is no longer the go-to place for millennials, you will need a Facebook business account to advertise on both Facebook and Instagram, so it's always recommended to have an account even if you aren't actively using it.

META Business Suite is the professional side of Facebook which every social media professional uses. One of the biggest challenges we see at Soar Media Group is when working with new clients or startups. They either don't yet have a META account or have tied a branded Facebook page to a personal account. It can be very messy when transferring ownership or advertising, so if you're starting fresh then you need to create a META Business Suite account.

Why use Facebook? Facebook has over 2 billion active users, making it a powerful platform for reaching a diverse audience.

X (Formerly known as Twitter)

X started as a short micro-blogging platform but has now become the go-to resource for on-demand news. Its largest demographic of users are between the ages of 25-35, and 17% of Americans get their news from X. Plus, more than 80% of X's global population is under the age of 50, so if you're marketing to millennials (25 to 40-year-olds) or Gen Z (12 to 27-year-olds), X may be for you.

Companies like Wendy's, MoonPie, and Gushers have all capitalized on meme culture on X and specifically targeted their content towards a younger generation. Making your content witty, funny, and slightly sarcastic may be an effective way to go viral and promote your product in a new way.

Speaking of Wendy's, they had a great example of an organic viral moment in 2017 when a fan tweeted at them and asked how many retweets he would need to receive a free year of their chicken nuggets. Wendy's promptly responded and challenged him to receive 18 million retweets. The challenge became a viral sensation as the world all turned to help the young fan achieve this goal, and at the time making him the most retweeted account in history. This campaign brought massive attention to Wendy's and was an organic, viral moment that helped them grow a larger audience on X.

All this said, X moves very quickly and needs to be nurtured with attention and content. If you don't have time to actively be there or aren't witty with words, it's best to direct your attention to a platform where you can be 100% active.

Why use X? X is known for real-time updates, news dissemination, and customer service interactions.

Pinterest

Pinterest has always been an interesting, semi-underground social media platform. Although it only garners users in the hundreds of millions (rather than billions like Instagram), Pinterest has a dedicated group of users who frequently visit the platform to share mood boards, recipes, and photos.

The largest demographic of users on Pinterest are millennial women, though Pinterest's Head of Business Marketing has claimed that men are the fastest-growing demographic. Pinterest is a very popular social media platform for people of all ages as 69% of their users are between the ages of 18-49.

Pinterest is photo-based, so companies will need a strong visual presence to inspire purchases on the platform. It acts as a great place for companies to link images from their websites, blog posts, and product pages. The platform can work especially well for fashion, home décor, and beauty-based companies.

A few years ago Pinterest integrated with Shopify to allow for in-app shopping, allowing users to view and purchase products directly. 40% of Pinterest users say that they are more likely to shop directly from the site, so adding this integration will also help your business.

Pinterest also sees an increase in users during specific seasons and holidays, like Halloween (227m searches), Winter (321m searches), and Summer (121m searches).

I personally use Pinterest to share all of my blog images and have success in generating traction. My outfit images are repinned monthly and I actively receive over 14,000 views a month. It's a very powerful awareness marketing tool, especially since most brands have no idea how to use it!

The reality is, if your brand is targeting women and you have strong lifestyle imagery, you need to be using Pinterest as a distribution platform.

Why use Pinterest? Pinterest is a visual search engine, making it suitable for inspirational and aspirational content.

YouTube

Let's get back to one of the titans of the industry, YouTube. We call it a titan for a reason as YouTube has billions of monthly users with nearly 1 billion videos watched per day! YouTube can be extremely beneficial to a business as 70% of viewers bought from a brand after seeing it on YouTube. Nearly 62% of businesses have a YouTube channel and it's the second most visited website in the world. Everyone in the world uses YouTube in some

TIP: If your brand is unable to effectively create high-quality videos on YouTube, consider sending your product to YouTube influencers so they can do the creative work for you.

capacity, but those 35 and under are the platform's largest demographic.

YouTube is a bit different from the other platforms as it's purely video-based, so companies need to make sure their content can be accurately translated to video. On the plus side, the ability to create a YouTube video is easier than ever, so it's important to focus on video quality to elevate your content above others.

YouTube has also grown into a vehicle for advanced storytelling, so be sure to focus on what your message is when making videos.

Why use YouTube? As a video-sharing platform, YouTube is excellent for storytelling, tutorials, and product demonstrations.

LinkedIn

LinkedIn has over 766 million active users and more than 70% of those users are outside the US. Unlike the others, LinkedIn's largest demographic is those between the ages of 46-55, but the new generation is on their way.

It's estimated that 46 million students and recent college graduates are starting to use LinkedIn, and make up the fastest-growing demographic on the platform.

LinkedIn is a great platform to connect directly with professionals in your industry and celebrate your accomplishments with a professional community. LinkedIn acts as a virtual, public resume/portfolio that you can use to show your audience your full potential and expertise in your field.

Why use LinkedIn? LinkedIn is tailored for B2B marketing and professional networking.

What is discovery commerce? Discovery Commerce is where your audience and potential followers find your brand via social media. Whether it be through Instagram, Facebook, or even a search engine. It is important to also fine-tune your SEO to make sure your brand is SEEN by the people you WANT to see your brand.

Chapter Summary

- Understanding what platform your target audience uses and aligning your platform choice with your business objectives are key factors in determining the best social media platform for your business.
- Considerations such as available resources for content creation, platform familiarity, and desired outcomes from social media usage are crucial in making an informed decision.
- Each platform has unique strengths, such as TikTok's viral potential, Instagram's e-commerce integration, Facebook's accessibility, X's news dissemination, Pinterest's visual appeal, YouTube's video-centric nature, and LinkedIn's professional networking capabilities.

CHAPTER 4

Revealing the Killer Social Media Strategy

When I first started writing this book I was trying to piece together a five page e-book. Little did I know I was going to quickly surpass that. The truth is, I have a lot to share after more than a decade in the industry. But more importantly, I wanted to piece together a book that also inspired and motivated a go-getter attitude.

The ***killer*** strategy is named to embody the idea of excelling in life, career, and social media.

The phrase "killing it" means performing exceptionally well at something or achieving great success. And that is exactly what the ***killer*** strategy shows you how to do.

There is a large database of evidence to show that social media marketing increases brand awareness, increases exposure to new audiences and helps increase sales. That said, a true return on investment (ROI) will never happen if you don't have a proper strategy in place.

While immediate boosts in followers, engagement, and views can be achieved with certain tactics, a comprehensive strategy ensures long-term success. Without a strategy, things can and will quickly fall apart.

So, let's dive into the ***killer*** strategy my team at Soar Media Group uses when managing and growing social media account for clients:

K. Know Your Audience

The foundation of any successful social media strategy lies in understanding your audience inside out. What makes them tick? What challenges do they face? What do you offer them that no one else can?

Armed with this knowledge, you can tailor content to resonate with your audience on a personal level.

TIP: You can't always be in two places at once, so plan to dedicate your time and energy into a platform that aligns best with your audience.

I. Invest in Content Marketing

Content is king, and investing in high-quality, value-driven content is non-negotiable. Content marketing has been the cornerstone of our agency's success. Whether it's captivating visuals, informative videos, or engaging audio clips, prioritize content that educates, entertains, or inspires your audience. Quality content grabs attention and fosters trust and loyalty. A single, well-crafted post that resonates with your audience is far more effective than five generic posts that add no value.

TIP: Develop a brand voice and aesthetic, and stick to it. Consistency in social media is key.

L. Listen to Your Community

Social media is a two-way street. Actively listen to your community's feedback, questions, and concerns. Engage in conversations, address their needs, and show genuine interest in their opinions. Building a strong rapport with your community will foster long-lasting relationships.

TIP: Find local people and influencers within your community who would enjoy your products or services and engage with them. Offer to send them products for free in exchange for social posts. Be realistic about your outreach during this time. It's important to focus on micro-creators (under 20K followers) or influencers who have used your product in the past and tagged you in stories. If you reach out to someone with 1 million followers, it's unlikely they will post for less than $6,000. Remember, word-of-mouth marketing is the most powerful way to sell your product or service.

Do this regularly and don't be discouraged if the first five people don't reply.

L. Learn from Your Competitors

Conduct thorough competitor analysis to gain insights into their strategies, content, and audience engagement. Identify gaps and opportunities in the market and use this knowledge to refine your approach. Learn from their successes and failures, but always strive to differentiate yourself and offer unique value.

TIP: Search competitors and engage with their followers, they will likely share the same interests and fit your brand's target market.

E. Engage Before You Sell

Effective social media marketing is about building relationships, not just making sales pitches. Prioritize engagement over promotion by actively interacting with your audience. Respond to comments, messages, and mentions promptly. Establishing trust and rapport lays the groundwork for successful selling down the line.

TIP: Keep a list of the individuals who engage with you regularly (comment, hashtag, mention, share, react, retweet, quote, and like your posts). You can tag them, mention them, and eventually reward them for their support!

R. Recycle What's Working

Leverage what's already working by identifying top-performing content and strategies, and repurposing them for continued success. Repackage popular posts into different formats, explore new distribution channels, or revisit successful campaigns with a fresh twist. By recycling what resonates with your audience, you maximize your impact while minimizing effort.

I know what you're thinking. That's it? This is the KILLER strategy? In a nutshell, yes. But on a deeper level, no. The next few chapters dive into each part of the KILLER strategy individually, with worksheets, tips, and real-life stories to help you take action on each one.

For now, I'm giving you just the tip of the iceberg.

But before we dive deeper into the strategy, there's another element of social media you need to know: setting goals. Goal-setting is the most important element of a social media strategy because it keeps you accountable.

> **TIP:** Consistency is important when it comes to social media. Once you find out what's working and a format that you like, invest 100% into that. It's so important to resist the urge to change direction every few months.

Setting Clear and Achievable Goal for Social Media

Setting goals for social media is like plotting a roadmap for your journey. It helps you stay on track and know where you're going. Clear and achievable goals provide direction, focus your efforts, and help you measure success.

When building out your KILLER social media strategy, you need to include goals.

Goal setting will provide:

Clarity and Focus: Goals provide clarity on what you want to achieve through social media. They help define your purpose and guide decision-making.

Measurement of Success: Goals serve as benchmarks to measure progress and evaluate the effectiveness of your social media efforts.

Resource Allocation: Setting goals helps allocate resources (time, budget, manpower) efficiently towards activities that contribute to achieving desired outcomes.

Motivation and Accountability: Clearly defined goals motivate teams and individuals, driving them towards a shared vision. They also hold stakeholders accountable for results.

Use the SMART framework. SMART is an acronym that stands for Specific, Measureable, Achievable, Realistic, and Timely. This is a framework most seasoned marketers use, whether it be for social media or for traditional marketing. The framework has been a keystone when developing strategies for decades because it helps ensure your marketing plan is realistic based on your budgets, timelines, and overall capabilities.

- **Specific:** Clearly define what you want to accomplish (e.g., increase Instagram followers by 20%).
- **Measurable:** Establish metrics to track progress and success (e.g., track engagement rate, conversion rate).
- **Achievable:** Set goals that are realistic and within reach based on resources and capabilities.
- **Relevant:** Ensure goals align with overall business objectives and contribute to strategic outcomes.
- **Timely:** Set a timeframe for achieving goals (e.g., increase website traffic by 30% in six months).

The Difference Between Goals and Objectives

Goals provide the overarching vision and direction for Instagram growth, defining desired outcomes such as brand visibility, traffic generation, or audience engagement. Objectives translate goals into specific, measurable targets that drive actionable steps and progress measurement.

ASPECT	*GOALS*	*OBJECTIVES*
Definition	Broad, overarching aspirations or outcomes	Specific, measurable targets contributing to goal attainment
Purpose	Provide direction and purpose	Drive actionable steps and measure progress
Scope	Visionary and qualitative	Concrete and quantitative
Measurement	Often qualitative or directional	Specific, measurable, and SMART
Examples	Increase visibility on Instagram	Increase Instagram Follower Base by 20% in 6 Months

Steps to Setting Social Media Goals

When you're setting goals for you social media the first thing you need to do is understand your audience. Define your target audience, their preferences, behaviours, and pain points.

Next, link your social media goals directly to your broader business goals. Are you trying to create brand awareness? Do you want to build a community? Do you need to update existing customers with an important message?

Once you identify what you're trying to do with social media, you need to determine which metrics (e.g., followers, engagement rate, purchases) will measure success.

Then, create an action plan. Develop tactics to help you achieve your goals, including content plans, advertising campaigns, and engagement strategies.

TIP: Don't be afraid to monitor and adjust. Regularly monitor progress, analyze data, and adjust strategies based on the insights you collect. It's okay if your tactics change once you see what actually works.

The Difference Between Objectives and Tactics

Many inexperienced marketers may struggle with understanding the difference between objectives and tactics due a lack of understanding and the pressure to deliver immediate results. To build a proper strategy, it's imperative that you understand the difference between these two and plan accordingly.

Objectives define desired outcomes, while tactics outline specific actions to achieve those outcomes. By setting clear objectives and implementing effective tactics, businesses can align their social media efforts with strategic goals, optimize resource allocation, and drive measurable results.

For example, if my goal is to build an active community of moms in my neighbourhood using Instagram, it would make sense to launch weekly giveaways that target moms. I could give away tickets to family-friendly activities, partner with brands that sell family-friendly products and partner with studios that offer mommy and baby classes.

My goal is to build a community, my tactic is to do this through partner giveaways.

ASPECT	*OBJECTIVES*	*TACTICS*
Definition	Specific, measurable goals to achieve	Specific actions or methods used to achieve objectives
Purpose	Establishes desired outcomes	Outlines how objectives will be achieved
Focus	What you want to achieve	How you will achieve what you want to achieve
Examples	Increase brand awareness by 20% within 6 months	• Run targeted Facebook ads to reach new audience segments • Boost social media posts with a $200 boosting budget per month • Identify five viral videos related to my niche and recreate them • Collaborate with like-minded brands for an Instagram giveaway
	Generate 500 new leads per month	• Add a 'book now' button to my social media profile • Offer a referral incentive to existing customers • Run targeted social media ads
	Improve customer engagement on Instagram	• Host interactive giveaways • Ask my audience insightful questions • Give my audience a sneak peek into a new product launch and ask their honest feedback

Chapter Summary

- Knowing your ideal customer helps you create effective social media content and messaging.
- Social media is social — don't be scared to speak to your community and engage with them directly. They will be your biggest asset when it comes to organic awareness.
- Your competitors provide high-value insights and should always be on your radar.
- Prioritize relationship-building over direct selling.
- Repurpose successful content and strategies to maximize impact while maintaining consistency.
- Setting clear and achievable goals provide direction, focus efforts, and measure success.
- Use the SMART framework (Specific, Measurable, Achievable, Relevant, Timely) to ensure that goals are well-defined and actionable, guiding social media strategies effectively.

CHAPTER 5

K. Know Your Audience

I once worked with a client who believed their product was for everyone.

That wasn't the case. When the client and their team marketed too broad, we saw campaigns flop. But when we tailored their messaging to men and women who were struggling with weight loss, who were diabetic, or were on a keto-friendly diet, we saw success.

Understanding your audience helps you tailor your product and messaging effectively. This is the most crucial step in the social media world and the only way to ensure you are creating social media content that appeals to your demographic and can create a positive return on investment (ROI).

You need to identify the people that are most likely to make purchases, promote your brand, and come back for seconds.

Not everyone on social media is driven to look at your business, and that's okay. To be successful, you've got to find the audience whose problem you are solving.

This is done by identifying your ideal customer based on demographics, interests, behaviours, and pain points.

For example, is your ideal customer a high-income woman who enjoys premium beauty products and is conscious of ingredients? Or is he a single man working an entry-level job who values budget-friendly fitness solutions?

Knowing your ideal customer helps you create effective social media content and messaging.

Before You Identify Your Audience

What Problem Are You Solving?

Successful businesses and products solve specific problems. Before identifying your target audience, it's crucial to understand the particular issue your product or service addresses. Knowing this with certainty ensures that your marketing efforts are directed toward individuals who will genuinely benefit from your offering. By pinpointing the problem, you can better identify and connect with the audience that needs your solution the most.

For example, Soar Media Group helps businesses that lack a creative or socially savvy team succeed on social media. We work with clients who don't have photographers, videographers, editors, or experienced project managers on their teams.

But let's assume you're in a different industry. Maybe you're a luxury real estate agent who specializes in helping clients get top dollar. To do this, you help them get show-ready. You work with a home stager and stage every home, you advise on new paint colours if needed and you maximize room layouts before the listing photos are taken. You also insist on lawn care before the property is listed. And you only work on homes that are worth more than 2.5 million dollars. Your country club network knows you. You are premium and they trust that when they need to sell their high-value home, you're the only person to do it.

In this example you have a clear understanding of who your ideal client is, what makes you different compared to other real estate agents and you know the problem you are solving: you help clients sell their high-value properties for top dollar.

Why Would Someone Be Interested In Your Product Over Others?

Consider the unique benefits and features that set your product apart. Understanding your competitive edge will help you articulate a compelling value proposition. This clarity will guide you in attracting and retaining the right audience who truly values what you offer.

For example, Soar Media Group offers a full-service team with over a decade of experience and a content-marketing-first approach. Our clients hire us because they know they will receive quality work that is intentional and backed by strategy.

Who Is Your Audience?

Now it's time to build out your ideal audience. Understanding your audience is crucial for crafting an effective content strategy and maintaining clear, targeted messaging. This worksheet will help you gain valuable insights into your target audience, and let you tailor your marketing efforts with precision.

Step 1: Demographic Profiling

Age Range: What is the age range of your ideal customer?

Gender: What is their gender?

Location: Where do they live? (Urban, suburban, rural, specific regions or countries)

Occupation: What types of jobs do they have?

Income Level: What is their average income or socioeconomic status?

Education Level: What is their highest level of education?

Step 2: Psychographic Profiling

Interests and Hobbies: What are their interests and hobbies?

Values and Beliefs: What values and beliefs are important to them?

Lifestyle: What does a typical day look like for them?

Personality Traits: What are their dominant personality traits? (e.g., adventurous, cautious, outgoing)

Attitudes and Opinions: How do they feel about topics relevant to your product or service?

Step 3: Behaviour Analysis

Buying Behaviour: How often do they purchase products like yours? Do they prefer online or in-store shopping?

Brand Loyalty: Are they loyal to specific brands? What influences their loyalty?

Pain Points: What problems or challenges do they face that your product/service can solve?

Decision-Making Process: What factors influence their purchasing decisions? (e.g., price, quality, recommendations)

Media Consumption: What types of media do they consume? (e.g., social media, blogs, podcasts, TV)

Step 4: Creating Buyer Personas

Persona Name: Give your persona a name for easier reference.

Demographics: Summarize key demographic details (from Step 1).

Background: Briefly describe their background, including job, family, and lifestyle (from Steps 1 & 2).

Goals and Needs: What are their primary goals and needs related to your product/service?

Challenges: What challenges do they face that your product/service can address?

Marketing Message: Craft a marketing message that speaks directly to this persona's needs, goals, and preferences.

Knowing who your audience is will make the difference between someone who is just posting to social media vs. someone who uses social media as a business tool.

Here are some additional strategies to help you identify your target audience:

Assess Customer Activity: Determine where your customers are most active. This could be specific social media platforms, forums, or other online communities.

Analyze Competitors: Observe who is engaging with your competitors. Identify what strategies are working for them and what pitfalls to avoid. Learning from their successes and mistakes can provide valuable insights for your business.

Use Website Analytics: If you have a website or online storefront, setting up Google Analytics is essential. Extract audience profiles to understand visitor demographics, behaviour, and interests. If needed, consider hiring a freelancer to help with this. Knowing your audience is a key component of an effective social media strategy.

Examine Social Media Insights: Use tools like Instagram Insights to gather data on the age, location, and gender of your followers. This information will give you a clearer picture of who is interested in your content.

Chapter Summary

- Successful businesses begin with identifying the specific problem their product or service solves.
- Highlight your unique benefits and features that resonate with customer needs.
- Use demographic, psychographic, and behavioural data to create detailed buyer personas. This helps tailor your marketing messages and strategies effectively.
- Regularly analyze customer behaviour, competitor engagement, and social media insights to refine and optimize your target audience strategy.

Take Action

Use the above worksheet to develop a detailed buyer persona. Remember, understanding your audience is key to driving engagement, conversions, and long-term business success.

CHAPTER 6

I. Invest in Content Marketing

Content marketing — the creation, distribution, and promotion of digital content to raise brand awareness or make a sale — is the single most important part of a social media marketing strategy. More and more companies are ditching traditional advertisements and opting to create a digital footprint by sharing content online, and rightfully so. With the internet in billions of shopper's hands, it's the only way to stay relevant.

Blogs, social media pages, and social media posts that link to your website all have the potential to make a sale.

Instagram, perhaps one of the most visual platforms aside from Pinterest and TikTok, now lets companies turn their social media posts into a digital storefront; consumers don't just view your content, they purchase from it.

Before you can create content, you need to understand what kind of content exists. These are the most common forms of content.

Photography (visual content)

Photography is one of the most common forms of content marketing. You see it used across Instagram, Pinterest, X, and Facebook; brands sharing high-quality images of their products to generate interest. Kylie Cosmetics does a great job of using photography to its fullest. Their Instagram feed enables consumers to purchase immediately after viewing an image. Kylie Jenner, the brand's founder, has been vocal about social media being her only form of marketing — creating a billion-dollar business from content marketing alone.

Videography (visual content)

Being the closest form of content marketing to conventional advertisements, videography is easily absorbable by viewers. Videos can range from product videos, to behind the scenes, to full-blown digital commercials. My favourite brand that has used video marketing from the start is GoPro. Their video content is shot on GoPros (genius, right?). Every video takes the viewer on an adventure, effectively showing what your life could look like if you owned a GoPro.

Whether it's featuring daredevils or everyday people, GoPro successfully shows their audience the incredible capabilities of their camera, while advertising the lifestyle that comes along with it.

GoPro takes this marketing tactic one step further by asking for user submissions filmed with the GoPro camera. What's in it for their followers? A chance to have their creative work reposted to millions of users. This kind of incentive leads to high engagement on social media, and a 'need it now' kind of mentality for anyone who loves to document their travels, adventures, or everyday life.

Graphics (visual content)

Social media graphics range from memes to quotes to infographics. The range is long and broad, but one thing they have in common is that graphics are excellent filler content. Filler content is when you don't have enough imagery or videos to share, so you communicate a valuable message in another medium.

The graphics we create at Soar Media Group change based on the client, but a good rule of thumb is if you can educate, inspire, or provide humour then a graphic is okay to post on social media.

A social media graphic is not and never should be a print ad. This is a rookie mistake I always see brands making.

Years ago, marketing teams defaulted to magazines, billboards, television, in-store displays and digital banner ads. As social media began to rise these teams had difficulty understanding how to navigate the landscape so they did what always used to work: posting ads on social media.

Unfortunately this doesn't work. Rather than communicating your message and getting users excited about your product or service, graphic advertisements come across as annoying.

With every graphic simply ask yourself this question: Do I use social media to look at things like this? What would I think if a different brand posted this? Would I engage, scroll page, or unfollow?

Usually, I unfollow.

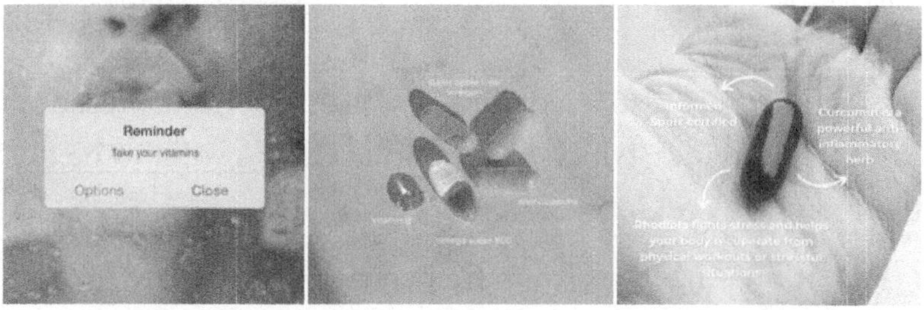

The above social media graphics were made for our client Platinum Naturals.

Podcasts (audio content)

Podcasts are digital audio files available for streaming or download, offering a convenient and versatile platform for content consumption. They provide listeners with on-demand access to a wide range of topics, from entertainment and education to news and storytelling. As a form of content marketing, podcasts offer businesses an opportunity to engage with their audience in a more intimate and conversational manner, building brand awareness and fostering meaningful connections.

Blog Posts (written content)

Blog posts are a great way to build SEO and bring users to your website. A brand that really leverages content marketing through blog posts is Whole Foods. Their blog perfectly addresses their demographic of men and women living healthy lifestyles. The blog shares healthy recipes, tips and tricks, shopping guides, and more. These blog posts show customers they are the experts in the healthy food sector and that they should be trusted with any and all healthy food needs.

Blog posts are also needed to establish an online presence on search engines, which is paramount if you want to be on the first page on Google.

When Soar Media Group first started out we used blogging as our primary driver of awareness. Each blog post we wrote was strategically chosen based on keywords and designed to bring people to our website. It worked. We generated two new business leads in a few months and one of those leads turned into a $300,000 client.

Customer Reposts and User-Generated Content (UGC)

Customer reposts are exactly what they sound like; reposts of images, videos, or reviews that your customers have taken. User-generated content (UGC) looks and feels like customer reviews, but it is usually paid for with a gifted product or monetary compensation to a lifestyle photographer or micro-influencer who will produce, shoot, and edit the content. Both of these forms of content are incredibly powerful in giving social proof.

Influencer Marketing

Influencer marketing isn't new, but it keeps growing. Brands use celebrity endorsements to gain a trustworthy brand presence and generate sales, but with social media anyone can become a celebrity. Instead of paying millions to an actress for one post, brands are finding success by partnering with influencers like fitness trainers living in rural America. This kind of marketing is effective whether consumers like to admit it or not.

Perhaps the most successful brand at influencer marketing is Revolve, the e-commerce retailer that began using influencers like Tuula Vintage, Negin Mirsalehi, and Song of Style before the rest of the world even knew what 'influencer marketing' meant.

Influencer marketing is so important that Financial Times has recently noted that influencers have the ability to make or break a brand — viral mentions and endorsements are now taken into consideration when buying or trading stocks.

What is the Difference Between an Influencer and a UGC Creator?

An influencer is an individual who has built a following and established credibility within a specific niche or industry. A UGC creator, or User-Generated Content creator, is an individual who generates content related to a brand or product, typically as a customer or fan of the brand.

What Do Brands Look For in Influencers?

The very first thing brands look for is whether or not the influencer fits their brand aesthetic. If I'm marketing for a food company and you only post outfits, it's unlikely I'll reach out.

Next, we advise our clients to look at the influencer's audience. Are they the people you want to target? Is there engagement? Is the engagement authentic? For example, a mommy blogger who only has other mommy bloggers commenting on her posts is a big red flag. We don't want other influencers. We want real customers who will purchase.

We also look at the quality of content. Is the amount you've quoted worth the reach and the quality of content? Can you produce something that is authentic and natural? Is your content high-quality?

Believe it or not, I've had a client pay tens of thousands for an iPhone photo, only to get a fraction of that return in sales. All this was without my consult. Don't be tricked by vanity metrics. Quality and authenticity will always reign supreme.

What is the Cost of Influencer Marketing?

The cost of influencer marketing can vary widely depending on several factors, including the influencer's reach, the scope of the campaign, and whether or not they have an agent. In general, someone who truly has influence (can generate purchases from promoting your product) can range from $1,500 - $20,000 per post.

It's important to distinguish whether or not you have the budget to work with an influencer or a UGC creator. In many cases, working with micro-creators (less than 20,000 followers), or UGC creators is more realistic for brands. Whichever you choose to do, remember that influencers are often considered 'top of the funnel' meaning they will bring awareness first, purchases second.

Creating Your Content

A big mistake brands make online is not sharing valuable content, and therefore not giving an audience a reason to stick around.

You need to evaluate your content and ask yourself '*What is my audience getting out of this? Why would they care? What am I giving to my audience that no one else can?*'

The more value you give, the more people will value your content. Here are some content categories that provide value:

- Information
- Entertainment
- Inspiration

This means you need to create content that either gives the audience information, is a fun piece of content, or offers them motivation/inspiration in their life.

Companies like Nike (inspiration), Wendy's (entertainment), and *Forbes* (information) all succeed on social media because they understand the value their content has and it helps them stand out from the crowd. Smaller brands are doing this very well too. Counterpart Brewing in Niagara Falls, Canada uses its social media to update its customers on their revolving menu.

Understanding what value you give your audience is key to a successful social media strategy.

Here are some examples of content that you can use to show more of your brand:

- Show off the lifestyle customers live with your product or service.
- Show your face, people want to see who they're following.
- Be open about your success and failures.
- Feature customers and users (often called UGC).
- Offer advice and information about your products.

What Is a Content Bank?

A content bank is a collection of images, videos, blog posts, and user-generated content that reflect your brand voice. These content pieces are stored in one place and can be shared throughout the year. You can choose to store them on your phone, in Google Drive, or use Dropbox (which is what we use for clients).

It is really important that you are confident these content pieces fit your brand voice and the quality of your brand. Anything that is unintentionally blurry or low quality should be removed. Social media users want to experience your brand the moment they land on your page and you want them to see the best of the best!

The assets within a content bank are used as a marketing tool and eliminate the stress of having to come up with content on demand. For example, having to search daily for a photo that flows well with your message isn't an effective use of your time.

Content banks also ensure that relevant content is being produced, posted, and repurposed for added value. It saves you time when planning your content calendar since you can focus on planning, and not creating.

These images are from a content bank that Soar Media Group created for Xhale Luxury Villa in 2017. We were on the frontier of content marketing and at the time, we were one of the only agencies in Toronto offering this service. Most agencies would use high-paying influencers for one content piece, rather than paying for a bank of content which is where the concept came from.

Content banks are a good investment for your overall marketing strategy, and something we start with for every new client. Not only are content banks a way to ensure you have assets that reflect a cohesive brand story, but they save you a tremendous amount of time when planning your social media calendar. Most social media burnout occurs from the pressure to continually create content. Remember what we discussed in Chapter 2? If you're burnt out, you can't be a good social media manager.

Though content banks are for internal marketing use only, you can distribute select assets to retailers or partners for additional exposure. For example, many of our clients at Soar Media Group sell their products in retailers across North America. We often share content banks with independent retailers when new products are launched so that they can also use branded photos and videos on social media.

How to Create Content That Resonates With Your Audience

After I bought my wedding dress, I met with my team to discuss my content plan. Of course I was getting married because I love my husband and wanted to celebrate with my closest friends and family, but I knew the day would be a huge opportunity for content creation. My team and I spent months planning ways to maximize the day for content creation, using the same process we would for any client.

First, we researched wedding content on Instagram and TikTok that did well. I wanted to see videos that had 500,000+ views and created discussion. What stories were being told? What parts of the day were most interesting for brides-to-be?

We created an outline of over 20 video concepts and scheduled the day accordingly. For example, the wedding was outdoors which meant we had a prime opportunity to shoot content at golden hour (the time right before and during sunset). I checked the sunset time using my weather app and noted it in the schedule: Get me from dinner at 7:00 p.m., no matter what is going on.

The result was a beautiful collection of sunset video clips and images.

After the big day, we slowly began to release the videos. Not surprisingly, three videos did exceedingly well, one going viral.

The first was 'What time did everyone arrive at my bridal suite.' This Instagram reel received 1.7million views and counting. It was focused on storytelling and gave a glimpse into the morning-of-the-wedding.

The second was 'Hits and misses at my wedding.' I shared what worked and what didn't so that future brides could get a completely unbiased opinion. The Instagram reel has half a million views.

The third was 'We practiced our wedding dance for months, only for my wedding dress strap to fall off during the big spin.' It was an authentic look into how important sticky tape is on the big day. Just kidding. It shared an authentic look at my husband and I spending hours practicing, and how important it is to plan for things that may go wrong. Fifty thousand people watched this Instagram reel.

My wedding content is a prime example of knowing your audience and creating content for them. Since the release I've had dozens of brides reach out to me with questions, and I was able to grow my community on Instagram by the thousands.

If there is one thing you take from this book, I hope it's this: You MUST know who your target audience is. Aside from talent and creativity, the most important element of creating content is understanding what your audience wants or needs. Do you know what they're interested in? Do you understand their pain points? Do you know WHY they are following you?

By knowing who your audience is, you can craft content that speaks directly to them, increasing engagement, loyalty, and ultimately driving conversions. Additionally, understanding your audience enables you to identify the most effective platforms, formats, and timing for your content, maximizing its impact and effectiveness.

Once you are confident in who your audience is, it's time to focus on the fun part: creating content. Here are the rules we follow at Soar Media Group.

Focus on Quality Over Quantity

Focusing on quality over quantity when it comes to content involves prioritizing the value and impact of each piece of content rather than the sheer volume of posts. The wedding videos I've listed above were all shot on an iPhone. Just because you're not shooting with $10,000 equipment doesn't mean you can't produce quality.

Quality content is relevant, relatable, and valuable to your audience. Understand your target audience's preferences, interests, and pain points. Tailor your content to address their needs and provide value.

Ensure that your content reflects your brand's voice, values, and identity. Consistency in branding helps build trust and recognition among your audience. Quality content reinforces your brand's reputation and strengthens its connection with followers.

Take the time to produce high-quality content that showcases your expertise and professionalism. Contrary to popular belief, you don't need fancy equipment to create quality content, but you do need a mild understanding of what makes something look and sound great. Here are some things you can do:

- Ensure your content is filmed or photographed with good lighting. I like to shoot in front of windows for natural lighting. Faux lighting takes a lot of skill and equipment to master, so it's better to avoid faux lighting if you don't have the experience working with it.

- Avoid blurry or messy looking content, unless this is intentional.
- If using audio, invest in a wireless microphone to avoid outside noise. These are usually between $100-$200 on Amazon and can make a huge difference in the sound quality.
- If creating Instagram reels or TikToks, focus on the first two seconds of your video. Use a catchy title to grab the attention of the viewer or save your best clip for the introduction.
- When shooting on an iPhone, always shoot in 4K as this setting allows you to crop your video without losing its quality.
- Use the Rule of Thirds. The Rule of Thirds is a photography concept that states that your subject or main focus should be in ⅔ of the frame. You can turn on the grid setting on your phone which will help with this.
- If creating an outdoor aesthetic, content shoot during golden hour for dreamy lighting.
- Focus on clean and simple shots. This is really important if you are just starting out. For example, if you are a hair stylist, I suggest shooting all of your clients in front of a window and against a simple backdrop like a wall, or go close up so the background doesn't distract the viewer.

- Include movement in every shot. Movement comes in different ways but the most common are: Zoom in, pan across, keep the camera still while things in your frame are moving like people walking, flower swaying, beverages pouring.

Quality content reflects positively on your brand and sets you apart from competitors.

Don't feel pressured to post content for the sake of it. Be selective and only publish content that meets your quality standards and contributes meaningfully to your social media objectives. Quality content is worth the wait and leaves a lasting impression on your audience.

By prioritizing quality over quantity, you can create meaningful connections with your audience, strengthen your brand presence, and achieve your social media goals more effectively.

TIP: Keep an eye out for trending audio with under 300 uses and jump on it for your next reel. It could give your content a nice boost!

Tell a Story

A great storyteller is genuine and authentic, sharing experiences and emotions in a relatable manner.

To be an effective storyteller you must first and foremost understand your audience. Think about what can resonate with their emotions, values, and interests. In the case of my wedding, I knew that brides-to-be romanticize the first dance because I just went through the process. I also knew they would care about what worked and what didn't because this is something I was obsessively researching in the year leading up to my big day.

Once you know what topic you want to talk about, use storytelling techniques such as a clear beginning, middle, and end, as well as effective transitions and pacing.

As with any great story, you need to focus on leaving an impact on your audience. Your goal should be to inspire, entertain, or enlighten your audience.

Give Value

Think about your favourite online creator. Why do you follow them? Do they give you outfit inspiration? Do they inspire you to decorate your home? Do they give you interesting recipes you never knew you wanted to try? Do they provide home maintenance reminders that help you maintain your home? Or maybe they share cute videos that brighten your day?

What all of those have in common is value.

Giving value in content marketing involves providing useful, relevant, and meaningful information or experiences

"Quality content reflects positively on your brand and sets you apart from competitors."

to your audience that address their needs, interests, or pain points. By consistently delivering valuable content that meets the needs and interests of your audience, you can build trust, loyalty, and engagement over time, ultimately driving business growth and success.

Here are my favourite ways to provide value:

Educate and Inform: Create content that educates your audience on topics related to your industry, products, or services. Provide valuable insights, tips, tutorials, how-to guides, or industry trends that help them solve problems or learn something new.

Entertain and Inspire: Capture your audience's attention by creating entertaining and inspiring content that resonates with their lifestyle. Use storytelling, humour, or motivational messages to evoke positive feelings and foster a connection with your brand.

Address Pain Points: Identify your audience's pain points and challenges, and create content that offers solutions, advice, or support. Address common questions, concerns, or misconceptions to demonstrate your expertise and build trust.

TIP: Look up search terms on Quora and Google to see what people are interested in. Popular topics on Quora show you that there is public interest in that topic. Always remember, social media is not about YOU, it is about your followers. Give them what they want, and they will give you what you want — an engaged audience that buys from you.

Provide Exclusive Content: Offer exclusive content, discounts, or promotions to reward your audience for their loyalty and engagement. Give them access to insider information, behind-the-scenes content, or sneak peeks that make them feel valued and appreciated.

Being Consistent with Your Social Media

Consistency in social media refers to maintaining uniformity and cohesion in the way content is presented across various platforms. This consistency helps establish brand identity, reinforces messaging, and enhances audience recognition. The easiest ways to be consistent on social media are:

Visual Style: Use consistent visual elements such as colours, fonts, graphics, and filters to create a cohesive look and feel across all posts. This helps reinforce brand aesthetics and makes your content instantly recognizable to your audience.

Content Formats: Maintain a consistent structure in your posts by using a similar format for captions, hashtags, and call-to-action (CTA) buttons. This makes it easier for your audience to engage with your content and understand your messaging.

Posting Schedule: Stick to a regular posting schedule to ensure consistency in the frequency and timing of your posts. This helps maintain visibility and engagement with your audience and establishes expectations for when new content will be available.

Content Themes: Establish consistent themes or topics for your content that align with your brand's values, goals, and audience interests. This helps maintain relevance and coherence in your messaging and content strategy.

Content Shoot Playbook

One of the biggest mistakes I see brands make is shooting content daily. This is completely impractical and an inefficient use of time. Instead, you should be planning a monthly, bi-monthly, or quarterly content bank where you can batch shoot and edit your content.

Here is the playbook we use at Soar Media Group every time we run a content shoot. We follow this same format for clients and for my personal brand, and I even followed this for my wedding.

Plan and Prepare

Create a detailed outline of what you're shooting, what it looks like, and what the final product looks like. When we shoot we have a very detailed outline that we follow so nothing is a surprise to ourselves or our clients.

Create in a Space That Matches Your Brand Aesthetic

We've used thousands of spaces — indoors and outdoors — and sometimes shoot at my home office. If you're creating product shots that don't need a lot of wide space

When managing the Children's Mental Health Ontario (CMHO) Instagram account we focused on using the company's brand colours for reels with one consistent font style throughout. This maintained consistency throughout the content and as the reels got more and more popular, it was evident exactly who was sharing them.

For this branded shoot, my team and I rented @nossostudio.ca which is a small but beautifully decorated space in East Toronto. Using a space that is already clean and fits your visual aesthetic saves time and makes content creation more efficient. We rented the space for two hours and were able to create 10 images and 10 reels.

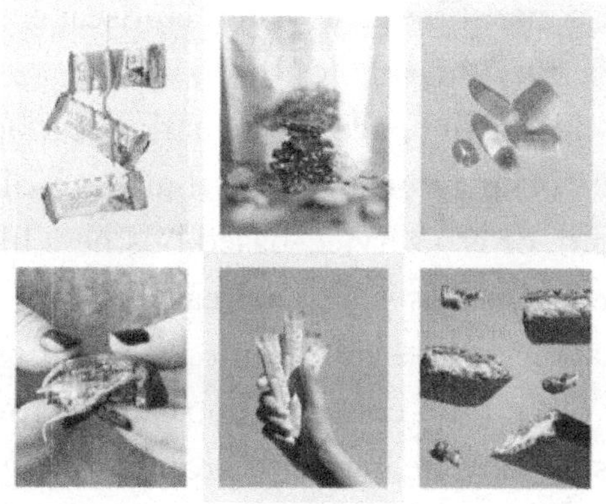

For simple product shoots like this, my team and I set up a studio in my home office. I like to use Club Backdrops for a variety of high-quality backdrops that are waterproof, and we generally set up alongside the window for natural light.

you can simply set up a corner of your home as a studio. Alternatively, if you're shooting with people or need to create a certain aesthetic using furniture or a setting, renting a space is a better option.

When planning a content bank I always scout spaces that fit the theme of the shoot. Some locations we've shot at include:

- **My home.** We use this space when running simple lifestyle or product shots since we have the set up and I've decorated my home with neutral furniture.
- **Studio spaces.** There are countless studio spaces available for hourly rentals. These are great for one-off shoots and/or if you don't have a studio space at home.
- **Outdoor gardens or parks.** The Niagara Botanical Gardens is one of my favourite spaces for spring

fashion content because of the landscape and shade, which acts as a natural diffuser.

- **Client offices or spaces.** This is the best option if you are working with a brand that has a physical storefront, or is a service-based business like a hotel, villa, or salon. This is also a great option if you are a real estate agent — your homes and listings are the perfect place for a content shoot and in most cases the space is already cleaned and professionally staged.
- **Co-working spaces.** East Room, for example, is an industrial co-working space with various buildings across Toronto.

Have Clear Roles Assigned to Team Members

When we create content we know who is shooting what, who is starring in what, and what role everyone has. This helps make content creation more efficient.

Even though we follow our content outline, we always allocate time for on-the-spot content. It's very common to get inspired with new ideas when you're on set. Let this creativity guide you.

Remember that efficiency should not compromise the quality of your content. Always strive to deliver valuable and engaging content to your audience.

> **TIP:** Shoot in front of a window for natural light. If shooting outside, look for spaces that are shaded to avoid overexposure or shoot during golden hour, the time right after sunrise or before sunset.

Never Stop Creating

Creating content is a long and sometimes arduous process. That said, you should never give up. Always create. Experiment with new formats and styles. Never stop creating. As you measure with analytics, you'll start to understand what's working and what's not. Use that to guide you, not discourage you.

TIP: Creating content that can be easily adapted across multiple platforms maximizes your reach and efficiency. You can do this by starting with a 'hero' piece of content that is more comprehensive like a Podcast episode, blog post, or YouTube video. Then repurpose this content across platforms by breaking it down into Twitter threads, Instagram carousel posts, and LinkedIn articles, and transforming key points into short, engaging videos for TikTok and Instagram Reels.

Content Shoot Outline

Content shoot date: ______________________

Schedule: ______________________

Team members on this shoot: ______________________

____

Props needed: ______________________

____

____

____

____

____

____

____

____

List 10 videos you will be creating, with examples to refer back to for styling or camera angle inspiration.

____

____

____

____

____

____

____

____

____

____

____

Chapter Summary

- Content marketing is crucial for establishing an online presence, staying relevant, and driving sales in today's digital landscape.
- Photography, videography, podcasts, blog posts, graphics, customer reposts, user-generated content (UGC), and influencer marketing are key forms of content used by successful brands.
- Content should provide value through information, entertainment, or inspiration, catering to audience interests and needs.
- Content banks offer a collection of images, videos, and blog posts that reflect brand identity and evoke emotion, streamlining content creation and ensuring consistency.
- Planning and preparation, space selection, role assignments, and flexibility are essential elements in executing successful content shoots.
- Never stop creating content and trying new things.

Take Action

Use the Content Shoot Outline to plan your next content shoot. Remember that your content needs to give value. Ensure that each of your videos offers advice, inspiration, or humour to your audience. If you need to film multiple takes of a video don't fret — it's perfectly normal to adapt and revise during a live shoot. You got this!

CHAPTER 7

L. Listen to Your Audience

In a bustling city like Toronto, standing out can seem nearly impossible. However, within your local neighbourhood, you're much more likely to get noticed. The same principle applies to social media. There's a common misconception that success depends solely on amassing millions of followers. Instead, focus on building meaningful engagement with your existing community right from the start.

In 2017, I launched Soar Media Group with a following of 5,000, yet my business continues to thrive, a demonstration on the significance of meaningful connections over sheer numbers.

This chapter delves into the critical importance of actively listening to your audience. Social media offers a direct platform for customers to voice concerns, ask questions, and seek support. Active listening gives you insights to create meaningful content that sparks conversations and encourages participation. It also empowers you to address feedback promptly, mitigating potential damage to your brand's reputation while strengthening loyalty and advocacy.

Listening to Strengthen Your Social Media Presence

While social media monitoring focuses on tracking specific metrics such as mentions, hashtags, or keywords associated with your brand, social media listening goes beyond mere data collection. Listening involves interpreting the data gathered, gaining insights into audience perceptions and preferences, and using these insights to inform strategic decisions. Monitoring is about observing; listening is about understanding.

Active social media listening offers a number of advantages, including:

Customer Insights: By actively listening, you can gain valuable insights into customer preferences, concerns, and expectations. This deep understanding allows for more targeted marketing efforts and product development.

Enhanced Customer Service: Proactively addressing customer feedback and concerns demonstrates responsiveness and improves overall customer satisfaction. This can lead to increased loyalty and positive word-of-mouth recommendations.

Crisis Management: Early detection of negative sentiment or emerging issues enables brands to address them swiftly, minimizing reputational damage and turning potential crises into opportunities for positive engagement.

Competitive Analysis: Monitoring competitor activities and customer conversations about competitors provides valuable benchmarking data. This helps brands identify gaps in the market and stay ahead of industry trends.

Content Strategy Optimization: Insights gained from social media listening can inform content creation strategies, ensuring that content resonates with the audience's interests and preferences, thereby increasing engagement and reach.

Brand Perception: Actively engaging with audience feedback and demonstrating genuine interest in their opinions helps build trust and foster a positive brand perception. This humanizes the brand and strengthens its relationship with customers.

Listening to Build a Community & Reach New Audiences

Effective engagement on social media can be categorized into proactive and reactive approaches.

Proactive engagement involves actively seeking out and initiating conversations with your audience, anticipating their needs, and fostering relationships before issues arise. In contrast, reactive engagement is responsive, focusing on addressing customer inquiries, feedback, or issues after they have been raised, often in real time. Balancing these strategies is key to maintaining a dynamic and responsive presence on social media.

Managing Incoming Messages and Mentions (Reactive Engagement)

Brands have significant opportunities to engage by responding to comments and acknowledging mentions in user content. This fosters one-on-one connections and builds brand loyalty, establishing a foundation for ongoing communication. This type of social media engagement fosters brand loyalty.

Managing these relationships may seem daunting, especially as your follower count climbs into the tens of thousands. However, don't let the prospect of increased engagement deter you. Engaging with your audience by addressing their questions and comments not only encourages interaction but also demonstrates your commitment to listening and valuing their input.

3 Tips to Managing Incoming Engagement (Reactive Engagement)

Engage with every comment on your posts. Feel free to ask questions to keep the conversation going or direct them to relevant sources if you don't have the answer.

- Respond promptly to direct messages to showcase excellent customer service.
- Maintain a record of individuals who consistently engage with your content (via comments, tags, or

likes). You can acknowledge them by tagging or mentioning them and consider rewarding their support in the future!

Monitoring Keywords Associated with Your Brand (Reactive Engagement)

Monitoring keywords related to your brand on social media is essential for staying informed about what people are saying and how they perceive your business.

To effectively monitor keywords, start by identifying relevant terms, including your brand name, product names, industry keywords, and common misspellings.

There are paid tools, like Hootsuite or Sprout Social, that monitor conversations, but I've always found keyword searches and alerts within social media platforms themselves are the most effective. For example, you can 'follow' hashtags in Instagram and look up keywords to find discussions.

"Monitoring is about observing; listening is about understanding."

Handling Negative Feedback and Customer Complains (Reactive Engagement)

As your social media brand grows there will be a time that you need to handle negative feedback.

I vividly remember being 24 and just a few months into my first role as a social media coordinator. Social media was still in its early stages, and my position had been newly created. One day, a crisis erupted, and the brand's social media pages were flooded with backlash. The team was caught off guard, unsure of how to respond.

The Director of Communications pulled me into his office with the Chief Marketing Officer and asked plainly, "What have other brands done in this case? What do we do?"

I replied, "Be authentic. Acknowledge the error. Promise to do better. Show that this is an isolated incident and you are taking it seriously with the utmost professionalism."

The response seemed to throw them both off their feet. Acknowledging it, they thought, brought more attention. But by the time our meeting was done it was clear there was no other choice.

The moral of the story is this: negative attention will happen. Social media crises will happen. And customers will forgive you if you stay authentic.

Handling negative feedback and crises on social media requires a thoughtful and proactive approach to maintain brand reputation and customer relationships. When faced with criticism or negative comments, it's essential to respond promptly and professionally. Start by acknowledging the feedback and expressing empathy towards the customer's concerns. This shows that you are attentive and genuinely care about resolving the issue.

Avoid getting defensive or dismissive, as this can escalate the situation further.

After acknowledging the feedback, take the conversation offline if necessary to address the issue privately and offer a solution. Provide contact information or invite the customer to reach out through direct messaging or email to discuss the matter further. This demonstrates a commitment to resolving the issue and shows other customers that you take their concerns seriously.

In the event of a social media crisis, such as a public complaint or negative viral content, it's crucial to act swiftly and transparently. Communicate openly with your audience. Be honest about the situation and take responsibility for any mistakes made. Implement a crisis communication plan that outlines key steps to mitigate damage and restore trust. By handling negative feedback and crises effectively, you can turn challenges into opportunities to strengthen brand loyalty and credibility.

Community Management & Actively Joining Conversations (Proactive Engagement)

My favourite part of social media marketing is proactive, because this is where the magic happens.

Proactive efforts are when you engage in conversation with influencers, followers, and followers of competitor brands to increase organic growth. This will be done through a combination of commenting, liking, and following people/brands that demonstrate your company's brand identity.

Proactive engagement is an easy win. And here's how to do it. For 15 minutes per day, interact with various accounts within your niche.

- Simply follow, like and comment on accounts and content that fits your target demographic.
- Users who use hashtags relevant to your niche, for example #womensstyle or #styleforwomen.
- Brands you would like to partner with.
- Explore your competitors and interact with their followers; chances are, they share similar interests and align with your brand's target audience.
- Commenting on viral videos or trending videos so that you can hit those people who are 'just here for the comments'.

TIP: Use the algorithm to your benefit. Commenting on your own post, responding to every comment, and asking friends and family to share important posts will give your content a boost.

Monitoring Branded Hashtags (Proactive Engagement)

Branded hashtags aren't as effective for awareness as they were in 2017, but they are a great way to categorize content about your brand. Encourage users who are sharing content about your brand to use your branded hashtags. This will increase word-of-mouth marketing and also help you find and engage with customer content.

Remember to interact with posts about your brand, even when the brand's handle isn't mentioned. You need to be social on social media.

Chapter Summary

- Focus on building authentic connections with your existing community rather than fixating on follower numbers.
- Actively tune into your audience's needs, preferences, and feedback to forge deeper connections, foster loyalty, and drive meaningful interactions on social media.
- Proactively engage with your audience through both proactive (initiating conversations) and reactive (responding to comments and mentions) approaches to maintain a dynamic and responsive social media presence.

Take Action

Create a list of key terms associated with your brand and set up alerts on your preferred social media management tool to begin monitoring conversations. Regularly review the conversations to gauge sentiment, identify trends, and engage with your audience proactively. This proactive approach not only helps in managing your brand's reputation but also enables you to capitalize on opportunities for engagement and growth.

CHAPTER 8

L. Learn from Your Competitors

When I first started Soar Media Group, there were few social media agencies offering content creation. I didn't have a good competitor list to analyze but that didn't stop me from thinking outside the box. Since my biggest competitors at the time were traditional PR agencies in the city, I used those PR agencies as references for building Soar's website and overall brand identity. I took note of what I visually liked and disliked and began to implement those insights into our overall branding.

For social media inspiration I would browse successful influencers and clothing brands, drawing on their content formats and Toronto-based keywords.

These competitor insights helped me elevate Soar Media Group's identity and digital presence. Within six months we were generating organic leads from clients finding our website and eventually our social media.

Whether you're a pioneer in your field or entering a crowded market place, you need to find competition you can draw inspiration from. Keeping an eye on your competitors is essential for staying up-to-date with new trends and monitoring changes in your industry. Watching what works for others and what doesn't helps you find effective ways to market yourself or your brand. You can replicate effective strategies that resonate with your audience while avoiding common pitfalls that may harm your brand's reputation.

Fast forward to now, and it feels like there are social media agencies everywhere. Social media marketing has become a crowded market place, or as I see it, an opportunity to learn and experiment. I encourage our social media manager to regularly look at other agencies in our space. Why ignore competition when they can instantly give us industry insights we may have missed?

As we've grown over the years I see new and creative competition emerge. This competition often inspires us to try new things or encourages us to be more aggressive. For example, in 2017 it was taboo to share a raw look into what running a business is really like. But now, audiences crave authenticity. We can see that when our competition shares raw and real insights their audience responds.

Viewing other agencies lets us see what is working (and not working) for them. Plus, it's the fastest way to find out if there is a new trend (leave it to a social media agency to find a trend first). The social media landscape is constantly evolving, and continuous improvement is key to staying competitive.

The moral of this strategy piece is this: Don't be afraid to support other businesses in your niche while you learn from them. Learning from competitors is a necessary stepping stone to social media success.

This chapter will guide you through the process of identifying, analyzing, and learning from your competitors on social media to enhance your own strategies and grow your online presence.

Insights You Can Gain From Competitors

Monitoring competitors helps identify gaps in the market or untapped audience segments. This allows you to capitalize on opportunities for growth and expansion within your niche.

By understanding how competitors position themselves and communicate with their audience, you can strategically differentiate your brand. This ensures your unique value proposition stands out in a crowded marketplace.

Insights gained from competitors can inspire new ideas for engaging content, promotions, or community-building activities. This enhances your ability to attract and retain customers through compelling social media interactions.

Regularly checking in with your competitors helps you avoid social media mistakes such as insensitive posts, inconsistent branding, or inadequate response to customer feedback.

How to Find and Monitor Your Competitors

Before diving into competitor analysis, it's essential to understand the different types of competitors. Direct competitors offer similar products or services and target the same audience. Indirect competitors may not offer the same products but target overlapping or adjacent markets.

To identify competitors on social media, start by researching businesses similar to yours that operate in your niche or geographical area. You can do this by typing your niche into Google, for example "hair stylists Toronto" and then make a list of all the brands that come up. Look for each of these brands on social media. To avoid overwhelm, pick the top three to five businesses to analyze.

Start by following your competitors on all relevant social media platforms. This ensures you stay updated with their latest posts, promotions, and interactions. Examine the type of content your competitors share. Are they posting images and videos, or sticking to one content type? Understanding their content strategy can help you identify what resonates with your shared audience.

Note how often your competitors post and at what times. Consistency and timing can significantly impact engagement levels.

Analyze the engagement their posts receive, such as likes, shares, comments, and overall interactions. High engagement often indicates effective content.

Notice how they foster a sense of community. Do they encourage user-generated content or do they shoot all content themselves?

Compare their audience demographics with your own. Identifying similarities and differences can help you refine your targeting strategies.

Observe how they maintain a consistent brand voice across different types of content. Consistency helps build a recognizable and trustworthy brand.

After you've finished reviewing your competitors' accounts, provide a step-by-step list on how you will incorporate the insights gained from competitor analysis into your own social media strategy. This might include adjusting your content plan, engagement tactics, or overall approach.

Questions to Ask Yourself When Looking at Competitors

There are countless ways to draw inspiration from your competitors but a good starting point is asking these questions:

- What content formats are working for them? Which content pieces have the highest views or engagement?
- What's not working for them and what can I avoid?
- How often are they posting?

- What is something new they've tried that I can draw inspiration from?
- What keywords and hashtags do they use?
- Do they do a better job of communicating their unique value proposition?
- Are they using influencers? If so, who?

Putting Theory Into Practice

Let's say you run a local beauty salon and want to enhance your social media presence by learning from competitors. Here's how you can put competitive analysis into action:

1. Start by identifying direct competitors in your area — other local beauty salons or hairdressers who target a similar demographic.
2. Analyze competitors' social media presence: Visit their social media profiles (Instagram, TikTok, etc.) and note their follower count, engagement rates (likes and comments), and frequency of posts.
3. Look at the types of content they post (e.g., before-and-after transformations, client testimonials, product showcases).
4. Identify successful strategies they use, such as behind-the-scenes videos showing services, or collaborations with local influencers.
5. Note effective use of hashtags relevant to their niche and local community.
6. Adapt successful strategies to fit your brand's style and offerings. For example, if a competitor uses client

testimonials effectively, start collecting and sharing your own client success stories.

7. Experiment with new content formats or engagement tactics inspired by what you've observed, such as offering exclusive promotions through Instagram Stories.
8. Track changes in their strategy and audience engagement metrics over time to stay updated on trends and adapt your approach accordingly.

By actively learning from competitors and implementing insights gained through competitive analysis, your local beauty brand or hairdressing salon can enhance its social media strategy, attract more local clients, and build a stronger community online.

Chapter Summary

- Understanding direct and indirect competitors, following their social media accounts, and staying updated with their activities is crucial to staying competitive in the ever-changing social media landscape.
- You can learn from your competitors by examining the type of content competitors post, their posting frequency, engagement levels, and multimedia use to identify successful strategies and pitfalls.
- Use insights from competitor analysis to adapt your social media strategy, avoid common mistakes, stay ahead of trends, and continuously improve your online presence.

Take Action

Start by identifying 3-5 direct competitors in your local area or niche. Make a list of three things they are doing well, and three things they aren't doing well. Select one of the things they are doing well at and implement it in your own social media. This could be a style of content, keywords they are using, or how they are leveraging platform features.

CHAPTER 9

E. Engage Before You Sell

For the first time in history, social media has given brands the ability to communicate directly with their audience. You can follow your customers, answer their questions directly, and thank them personally for supporting your brand. Think about it, what other marketing outlet lets you actively check in on your customer's lives?

Effective social media marketing isn't just about making sales pitches; it's about creating a community where your audience feels heard, valued, and understood. In fact, one of the most powerful outcomes of prioritizing engagement is the ability to create a community.

This community-building approach was exactly how we grew one of our clients from 0 to 19,000 Instagram followers in three years and over $60,000 in website sales per month.

As we saw more customers tagging the brand in social media posts, we decided to follow them. This audience in particular was heavily focused on weight loss and documenting their journeys online to stay accountable. I took the lead in checking in on them every week. I would like their posts, comment on their achievements, and send them personal messages of encouragement.

Then, when new products would drop, I would ship them free bundles of the product to try.

In months these customers became top advocates of the brand. I watched them spend thousands of dollars on products, then create testimonial videos, share countless social media posts and encourage everyone from their own network to shop the brand's products. At one point, I even saw them jumping in to defend the brand when a negative comment would come in.

When the COVID-19 lockdowns finally came to an end, I advocated for 10 of these customers to come to a private launch party in Toronto. They were the only public patrons invited.

At the party they shared even more content and celebrated the brand's launch alongside the founder. At one point, two of them took me aside to tell me they were 'so proud of how the brand had grown.'

They felt that the brand's success was their own. They felt they were part of a community.

Many brands fall into the trap of using their social media platforms solely for promotion. While it's tempting to focus on driving sales, prioritizing engagement can yield greater long-term benefits.

Actively interacting with your audience by liking, commenting, and sharing their content helps humanize your brand and builds a stronger connection with your followers. This can also make your brand more relatable and trustworthy. When your audience feels like they're part of a community, they're more likely to become loyal advocates for your brand.

Meaningful relationships with your audience trump traditional marketing every time.

Building trust takes time, and this trust is cultivated through consistent, genuine engagement. Sharing valuable content, answering questions, and providing insights without always pushing a product shows that your brand is not just interested in making sales but also in contributing value to your audience's lives.

Regular engagement helps your audience feel connected to your brand, making them more likely to turn to your brand when they need the products or services you offer.

TIP: Respond Promptly! In the digital age, customers expect fast responses. Responding quickly to comments, messages, and mentions shows that you care about your audience and are committed to providing excellent customer service. This attentiveness helps build a positive reputation and fosters trust.

Sell Solutions, Not Products. And Do It Authentically.

One crucial aspect of engagement is shifting the focus from you to them. You're not just selling a product, you're selling a solution to someone's problem.

All-inclusive resorts sell relaxation.

Supplement companies sell health and wellness.

Luxury car brands sell status.

When you present your product as a solution, sales naturally follow.

Prioritizing engagement over promotion means actively interacting with your audience. By engaging with your audience, you gain insights into their challenges, needs, and desires, allowing you to tailor your messaging to highlight how your product solves a specific problem they face.

But engagement alone isn't enough. To truly connect with your audience, you must also be authentic. Gen Z and millennials, in particular, place a high value on authenticity in the brands they support. They're more likely to connect with and buy from brands they perceive as genuine and transparent. In fact, studies show that 90% of consumers, especially younger ones, prioritize authenticity when

> **"You're not just selling a product, you're selling a solution to someone's problem."**

choosing which brands to support. This means they want to hear real stories, including the founder's journey or customer experiences they can relate to.

Sharing these authentic stories helps create a deeper connection with your audience, making them more likely to engage with and support your brand. When you engage before you sell, you're inviting your audience to be part of your brand's story.

So how do you do this?

The formula we use at Soar Media Group to foster a community is so simple, it's almost incomprehensible. Many times clients will think vanity metrics like hundreds of thousands of followers is the only way to make sales, but this isn't the case. A small community that trusts your brand is more effective than three hundred thousand followers who forgot they were following your account.

Here is the formula we use to drive sales on social media:

Building relationships + establishing trust = creating a community

An engaged community = long-term sales

TIP: Keep a list of the individuals who engage with you regularly (comment, hashtag, mention, share, react, retweet, quote, and like your posts). You can tag them, mention them, and eventually reward them for their support!

To do this, you first need to focus on understanding your customer's needs. Through consistent engagement, you can learn what your audience truly needs and how your product can meet those needs. This approach helps in crafting messages that resonate deeply with your audience, making your product more appealing as it's seen as a solution rather than just another purchase.

Second, position your product as a solution. When you engage with your audience, you can position your product in a way that directly addresses their pain points. Instead of saying, "Here's what we sell," you can say, "Here's how we can help you." This subtle shift in messaging can significantly impact how your audience perceives your brand.

The Gen Z and Millennial Perspective

Authenticity is more than just a buzzword, it's a necessity, especially when targeting Gen Z and millennials. These generations value real, relatable stories and are more likely to engage with brands that showcase transparency and authenticity.

- According to a survey by Stackla, 86% of consumers say authenticity is important when deciding what brands they like and support. For Gen Z and millennials, this number is even higher.
- A study by Sprout Social found that 90% of consumers believe authenticity is crucial in deciding

which brands they like and support, with 85% specifically mentioning they would only support brands they perceive as honest and authentic.

- Additionally, 62% of Gen Z and millennial consumers want to hear the founder's story or the real story behind a brand, according to a report by Edelman.

These statistics highlight the importance of weaving authentic narratives into your brand's story.

Instead of posting boring product photography, try sharing the founder's journey, company values, or real customer stories. Dive deep and share the story of how your brand came to be, the challenges you've overcome, or the values you stand for.

Customers don't just want to know what you sell, they want to know who you are, what you believe in, and why you do what you do.

Remember, real stories make a real impact.

To expand beyond the brand's story, encourage your customers to share their stories, experiences, and testimonials. User-generated content that reflects real-life use and satisfaction with your product is more influential than any ad you could create. It's relatable, genuine, and shows your product solving real problems.

Tips for Engaging Effectively

To engage effectively, personalization and acknowledgment are key. Your audience wants to feel like they're interacting with a real person, not just a brand. Tailoring your responses to individual users can make a big difference. Whether it's using their names, referring to past interactions, or acknowledging their specific concerns, personalized responses make your audience feel valued and appreciated.

For example, instead of replying to a regular customer with an emoji, you can say something like "Thank you for your ongoing support Heather!"

Another effective way to engage your audience is by rewarding their engagement. Acknowledging and rewarding your most active followers is a powerful way to maintain and increase engagement.

Hosting giveaways, offering exclusive content, or featuring user-generated content on your platforms show appreciation and encourage further interaction.

Lastly, keep a list of individuals who engage regularly with your brand. This could include those who frequently comment, hashtag, mention, share, react, or like your posts. Tag them in posts, mention them in comments, and create shout-outs to show that you appreciate their support.

"A small community that trusts your brand is more effective than three hundred thousand followers who forgot they were following your account."

This not only strengthens your relationship with these individuals but also encourages others to engage more frequently.

Handling Negative Feedback

Engaging with your audience also means handling negative feedback constructively. Addressing criticism or complaints on social media provides an opportunity to show your brand's commitment to customer satisfaction. When handled well, a negative situation can be turned into a positive experience, demonstrating your brand's dedication to resolving issues and valuing customer feedback.

Responding to negative feedback in a respectful and constructive manner not only helps retain customers but also shows potential customers that your brand is reliable and trustworthy.

TIP: Have a clear plan for addressing negative comments or reviews. Respond promptly, offer solutions, and always aim to turn a negative experience into a positive one.

Using Insights to Enhance Interaction

Engagement isn't just about responding to comments or messages, it's also about understanding what resonates with your audience. Social media analytics can provide valuable insights into what type of content your audience engages with the most. By regularly reviewing engagement metrics (such as likes, comments, shares, and the time of day when engagement is highest), you can refine your content strategy to focus on what works best.

Using data to drive engagement allows you to be more targeted in your approach, ensuring that your efforts are focused on creating content that your audience will find valuable and engaging.

> **TIP:** Regularly review your social media analytics to identify trends and patterns in your audience's behaviour, and adjust your content strategy accordingly to maximize engagement.

How Do You Balance Automation and Authenticity?

Automation tools can be incredibly helpful for managing tasks like scheduling posts, sending automated responses, or gathering data. However, it's crucial to maintain a balance between automation and authenticity. While automation can save time, it should not replace genuine interaction.

Your audience can tell when they're interacting with a bot rather than a real person, which can undermine the authenticity you've worked hard to build.

> **"When you engage before you sell, you're inviting your audience to be part of your brand's story."**

To maintain this balance, use automation for routine tasks like scheduling your posts and stories, but always prioritize personal engagement when it comes to direct communication with your audience. This ensures that while your brand is efficient, it also remains personable and relatable.

Real Life Examples: Brands That Engage Before They Sell

Starbucks

Starbucks is a great example of a brand that has effectively engaged its audience before pushing sales. Their #RedCupContest, which encourages customers to share photos of their holiday themed cups, has become a tradition that engages customers and builds community without directly pushing sales.

Glossier

Glossier is another brand that has built a strong community by prioritizing engagement over sales. They regularly interact with their audience on social media, asking for product feedback, sharing user-generated content, and even involving their followers in product development decisions. This approach has fostered a loyal customer base that feels like they're part of the brand's journey.

Chapter Summary

- Focus on authentic interactions. Make it a priority to engage with youraudience in a genuine, authentic way. Respond to comments, messages, and mentions promptly, and share your brand's story in a way that resonates with your audience.
- Build a community. create spaces where your audience can connect with each other and with your brand. This could be through exclusive online groups, live events, or encouraging user-generated content.
- Leverage data for engagement. Regularly review your social media analytics to understand what content resonates with your audience. Use this data to refine your content strategy and maximize engagement.
- Balance automation with authenticity. Use automation for routine tasks, but ensure that direct interactions — such as responding to comments or messages — are handled by a real person to maintain authenticity.
- Handle negative feedback constructively. Develop a plan for responding to negative comments or reviews. Aim to turn negative experiences into positive ones, showcasing your brand's commitment to customer satisfaction.

Take Action: Enhance Your Engagement

Step 1: Evaluate Current Engagement Levels

Review your current engagement metrics, including comments, likes, and shares. Identify areas where engagement could be improved, such as posts that received less interaction or times when response rates were slower.

Step 2: Implement a Response Strategy

Set a goal to respond to every comment and message within a specific timeframe, such as 24 hours. Create a content calendar that prioritizes engagement-focused posts, like polls, questions, or user-generated content, to encourage interaction.

Step 3: Build Your Community

Start building a list of regular engagers by tracking those who frequently interact with your posts. Develop a plan to tag, mention, and reward them over the next month to maintain their interest and encourage more engagement.

Step 4: Share Your Story

Dedicate time to crafting and sharing the founder's story, or the journey of your brand. Highlight real stories from customers who have benefited from your product, showing the human side of your brand.

Step 5: Test and Adjust

Test different engagement strategies, such as personalized responses, giveaways, or shout-outs. Monitor what resonates most with your audience and adjust your approach accordingly to maximize engagement.

CHAPTER 10

R. Recycle What's Working

When I first began sharing my life on social media, I spent countless hours brainstorming, filming, and editing fresh content, always striving to present something new to my audience. It was a labour-intensive process, and while innovation is important, I slowly realized that I was overlooking a goldmine sitting right under my nose — my existing content library.

One day, while scrolling through a home décor account I loved, I noticed a recurring pattern. The account owner shared the same clips over and over again, yet it never felt boring. She would tweak the text on the video, the overall message, or sometimes just edit the footage in a new and exciting way. This observation was an eye-opener. I realized that her audience was responding not just to new ideas but to the core messages and styles that resonated with them, even if they were repeated in different formats. It was then that I understood the importance of recycling content.

Recycling content doesn't mean being lazy or unoriginal. Instead, it's about recognizing the value in what you've already created and giving it a new life. By reimagining and repurposing content that has already proven successful, you can engage your audience in fresh ways without reinventing the wheel every time. It's about leveraging past success to fuel future growth.

This approach not only saves time and resources but also ensures that your message reaches a broader audience. Additionally, it allows you to build on the trust and engagement you've already established, reinforcing your brand's identity and message consistently.

In this chapter, I'll share strategies on how you can identify high-performing content, rework it to maintain its relevance, and adapt it across different platforms.

By recycling what works, you can maximize your content's reach and impact, creating a sustainable and effective content strategy. Let's dive into the art of recycling content and how to make the most of what you've already created.

Recycling Content

Recycling what's working on social media involves identifying successful content and strategies and then repurposing or iterating on them to maintain engagement and growth. By analyzing metrics such as likes, shares, comments, and overall reach, you can pinpoint which types of posts resonate most with your audience. Once identified, these successful elements can be used as a foundation for new content.

For example, if a particular video format or topic receives high engagement, consider creating a series or expanding on the theme.

Additionally, revisiting and updating high-performing content can keep it relevant and engaging. This iterative approach not only maximizes the value of your efforts but also ensures a consistent stream of content that aligns with audience preferences, ultimately driving sustained growth and success on social media.

Recycling content is also a great way to save on costs. This is because the effort invested in creating high-quality content is maximized by reusing and adapting it for different formats and channels.

Moreover, recycling content allows you to maintain a steady flow of valuable content without overextending your resources, making it an essential strategy for any content creator or marketer.

The Three Rules of Recycling Content

Recycling what's working on social media doesn't mean you should avoid trying anything new. It's about finding a balance between leveraging proven content and experimenting with fresh ideas. By mixing recycled content with new innovations, you keep your audience engaged and your content strategy dynamic.

1. Recycling successful content helps maintain consistency in your messaging and brand identity, which is crucial for building a loyal audience.
2. Recycling doesn't mean you need to stop innovating. Instead, explore new formats, topics or approaches. This allows you to attract new followers and keep your current audience engaged.

Recycling content requires you to test and learn.

What Does Recycling Content Look Like?

Recycling social media content involves repurposing existing material into fresh formats. Let's use Instagram as an example of how you can do this.

- **Original content that performs well:** A house tour video.
- **Recycled content part 1:** Break that video down into a quick and snappy tour of each room with additional aesthetic clips added.
- **Recycled content part 2:** Make a carousel post with images from each room.
- **Recycled content part 3:** Re-edit the original footage to a new sound. Revise video clips so they are shorter or longer and feel new. Add text 'POV: You've found your dream home.'

By recycling content in the ways described, you can keep your Instagram feed engaging while maximizing the value of your original content.

For example, if before and after videos do well for you, focus on sharing more content like this with the same editing style as you did the first time. There's no need to reinvent the wheel. You know what's working and you can capitalize on it.

At Soar Media Group, we've identified that office memes perform well. They add personality to our company and generate views. So we regularly sprinkle this style of content into our social media.

Evergreen Content

Evergreen content refers to content that stays relevant over time, regardless of seasonality. Unlike timely or trending content, evergreen content remains valuable throughout the year. For example, music award memes are only relevant for a few days after the live event. On the contrary, b-roll featuring your product or office space can be used year-round. How-to guides or before and after images are timeless.

If you are strapped with resources or budget, evergreen content is the most strategic kind of content to focus on. This is because you can recycle evergreen content over and over again.

To identify evergreen content, you need to first identify the content that your audience cares about. Look for high-performing posts, frequently asked questions, and content that consistently gets likes or comments. Remember when we talked about listening to your audience? This is the time to do it. Listen closely and they will tell you what content deserves to be recycled.

Formats for Recycling Content

Recycling content can take many forms, each suited to different platforms and audience preferences:

- **Static Posts:** Adapt photos and infographics into new static posts. These can be used for carousel posts, quote graphics, or themed collections.
- **Video Content:** Break down longer videos into shorter clips, highlight reels, or create new content like tutorials and explainer videos.
- **Stories:** Convert key content into engaging story highlights or series. Use story features like polls, questions, or interactive elements to boost engagement.
- **Carousels:** Turn detailed information or step-by-step guides into multi-slide posts that allow for a deeper dive into the topic.
- **Reels and Shorts:** Create short, snappy videos from longer content to capture attention quickly and align with trends.

No One Does It Better Than The Dave Ramsey Show

Dave Ramsey, a financial expert and radio host, effectively recycles content from his podcast. He repurposes podcast episodes into various formats such as short video clips, blog posts, social media updates, and email newsletters.

This strategy has significantly expanded the reach of his content. For example, key insights and popular segments from the podcast are shared as bite-sized clips on social media, which drives more traffic to the full episodes. This approach has contributed to a substantial increase in both listener engagement and subscriber numbers, something that Dave Ramsey often discusses in various episodes.

He has also used his main podcast discussions to launch micro-podcasts that are updated regularly. For example his shows The Ranmsey Show Highlights and Real Estate the Ramsey Way both use clips from his main show — he doesn't reinvent the wheel and rarely creates new discussions. He simply uses discussions and content he already has, but frames it in a new way that makes it feel exciting and new.

Best Practices for Recycling Content

To ensure recycled content is effective and engaging, follow these best practices:

- **Maintain Quality:** Ensure that recycled content maintains high quality and continues to offer value. It should be well-crafted and relevant to your audience.
- **Update and Refresh:** Revise any outdated information and update visuals or data to keep the content current and useful.
- **Consistency:** Align recycled content with your brand's voice and style to maintain a cohesive presence. Ensure that the recycled material feels fresh and consistent with your overall content strategy.

Chapter Summary

- Recycling content is about leveraging what works, not about being unoriginal.
- Identify high-performing content and repurpose it to extend its reach and impact.
- Recycling content saves time and resources, making it a cost-effective strategy.
- Balance recycling with innovation to keep your content strategy dynamic and engaging.
- Evergreen content is ideal for recycling because it remains relevant over time.
- Follow best practices to maintain quality, update content, and ensure consistency across platforms.

Take Action

Create a list of the top five pieces of content that you want to recycle. Write down the titles, themes, or descriptions of these posts, along with the metrics that made them stand out. This could be anything from a specific video that went viral to a post that got a lot of comments. Think of at least two new ways to repurpose each piece of high-performing content.

CHAPTER 11

Becoming a Killer Social Media Manager & Building Your Content Calendar

If I made a video called "Things I'd tell you if I wasn't afraid of your feelings," I'd start with this: the CEO's 14-year-old daughter is not a social media manager.

And neither is your cousin who's "good with her phone."

Somewhere along the way, the title social media manager became a catch-all for anyone who knows how to post. But a real social media manager isn't just posting. A real social media manager is building, shaping, and protecting the visual identity and community of a brand.

They're the person who turns comments into conversations, messages into insights, and strangers into a community.

A killer social media manager doesn't show up to "post on the feed."

They show up to understand the people behind the screen — their desires, fears, pains, habits, and motivations — and then build content that speaks to them so clearly that it feels personal.

And this is the part no one tells you. Or even acknowledges half the time. But it's the entire job.

Some of the biggest mistakes social media managers make include:

- **Lack of a clear strategy:** Not having a well-defined social media strategy can lead to inconsistent messaging, wasted resources, and ineffective campaigns.
- **Ignoring audience engagement:** Failing to respond to comments, messages, and mentions can alienate followers and damage brand credibility.
- **Overlooking analytics:** Neglecting to track and analyze social media metrics can result in missed opportunities for optimization and growth.
- **Inconsistent posting:** Irregular posting schedules can cause followers to lose interest and engagement to decline.
- **Posting ads as content:** Inexperienced social media managers often post ad creative as singular posts. This is the number one way to lose followers and lose engagement.
- **Not staying up-to-date with platform changes:** Social media platforms frequently update their

algorithms and features, so it's crucial for managers to stay informed and adapt their strategies accordingly.
- **Lack of authenticity:** Overly promotional or inauthentic content can turn off followers and hinder community growth.
- **Focusing on quantity over quality:** Prioritizing the quantity of posts over their quality can lead to content fatigue and decreased engagement.

Before You Post

Step 1: Determine Your Goals and Objectives

You need to set goals for your social media. You need to determine what you want to get out of your social media and how you are going to achieve this. Goals should be SMART – specific, measurable, achievable, realistic, and timely. This is key in selecting goals that can work for you.

For example, if you're a one-man show with numerous tasks on your plate, expecting to grow to 1,000 followers in one week may not be realistic. It's important to set yourself up for success by choosing goals that you're confident you can achieve.

Some goals you may have are:

- Post three times a week
- Engage with others in my industry
- Show off client work and use social media as a digital portfolio
- Raise awareness and generate client bookings

- Drive more traffic to my website
- Post a reel every day and generate at least 1,000 views from one reel
- Grow by 100 followers each month
- Gain 10,000 followers in three months

Outline your goals on a quarterly and monthly basis and always measure back. Make sure your tactics work alongside these goals.

Step 2: Identify Your Content Pillars

Content pillars are 3 to 5 topics your brand will consistently discuss, amplify, and create content for on social media. Content pillars vary drastically depending on the industry your business is in, but some examples include educational content (tutorials, about the product graphics, expert advice, ours vs. theirs), social proof (customer reviews, user-generated content (UGC)), sales and promotions, trends/memes/pop culture references, giveaways.

Step 3: Build Your Content Calendar

A content calendar is a guide for your social posts across all platforms. It includes the image or video to be posted, the caption, and a note about which social media platform to share it to. Preparing your social calendar for the month or two in advance can help you plan your social media strategy better and keep you organized. All professional social media managers make a content calendar and plan this in advance.

At Soar Media Group we plan our client content calendars a minimum of a month in advance, with a yearly forecast of all the important dates or campaign launches we need to plan for.

This is the checklist we use at Soar Media Group when planning a social media content calendar:

- ☐ Determine important promotions, campaigns, or dates that need to be integrated into the content calendar.
- ☐ Look at the yearly dates calendar and integrate any special days that are relevant.
- ☐ Look at the content pillars and determine what content is left to create for the month.
- ☐ Browse through assets on Google Drive, Dropbox, Canva or wherever you store your content bank.
- ☐ Put images on an Instagram layout (which you can create via Canva or Photoshop) to see if your calendar aesthetically looks good together. Don't be afraid to move around images that may not go well side-by-side. The only content that should be set in stone is content surrounded around a specific launch or a specific holiday.
- ☐ After you feel that your visual brand identity is accurately captured, add captions for your calendar. Try to avoid using any AI programs as much as possible. People don't want to hear a robot brand, they want your brand. Authenticity will always reign supreme.

- ☐ Add emojis to your captions to make them more fun and engaging, but only if it's on brand.
- ☐ Note important accounts you need to tag for extra awareness or collaborations.
- ☐ Make changes as necessary and adapt as necessary. Review captions and graphics for grammar, style, and brand voice.
- ☐ Schedule posts using a platform like META Business Suite, Iconosquare, Hootsuite or the platforms themselves. All posts on X, Facebook, and Instagram can be pre-scheduled in-app.

Planning out your social calendar in either a monthly calendar grid or chronological document will be the most effective. Social media is visual, so it's advantageous to plan your calendar in a visual manner.

Important Things to Keep in Mind When Planning Your Social Calendar

Schedule or post at optimal times

Studies conducted by social media planning, scheduling, and analytics software have identified optimal posting times for each social media platform based on audience engagement metrics such as views and impressions. While content no longer follows a strictly chronological order, it remains crucial to schedule posts on Instagram during peak times to maximize audience reach.

Benefits of creating your social calendar one month in advance

- Saves you time by pre-planning what you will post.
- Allows you to holistically see what messaging might be missing or what doesn't feel on-brand.
- Keeps you organized.
- Helps you plan for the future. For example, are you a chocolate brand and you missed National Chocolate Day? Or did you forget that International Women's Day was coming up and are now scrambling to figure out what to post? Professional social media managers are always one step ahead and they do this by planning their content in advance.

Your peak time will vary depending on your brand and geographic location, but a good rule of thumb is to post when people used their phones the most, which is after work (4 p.m. to 6 p.m.) or before bed (8 p.m. to 9 p.m.). Avoid sharing important messages on long weekends with good weather since most people will be off their phones.

Use keywords in your caption

There is growing evidence to suggest that social media platforms are using keywords in captions to categorize and find content. Mix up your social media captions using some short and some long, and experiment with including keywords about your content or account.

Be authentic

Take the time to find your voice and style. Followers can feel and sense when the content is forced, uncharacteristic, or impersonal. Social media should be social, it's important to convey your story in your own way to best connect you with your true audience.

Provide value

Think about what value you're providing your audience. Are you teaching your followers something useful? Are you entertaining them with humour or storytelling? Are you inspiring them?

Use the 80/20 rule

The 80/20 rule is a marketing adage that suggests 20 percent of your content should sell while 80 percent of your content should inspire.

Using hashtags

I always tell clients, "If someone told you they know how to make you go viral they are lying." Well, the same is true for hashtags. If someone tells you there is one-size fits all, they are lying. Either that or they have no real-world experience running social media accounts.

Some social media experts say only use three hashtags while others will tell you to stuff dozens into a comment underneath your post. The truth is, you need to experiment to find out what is working for you.

Start with key words and phrases relevant to the content you are posting about. Look through the most popular posts that use those key words and phrases and find out what other hashtags they use that are relevant to your content.

Find what's trending by searching keywords in the Instagram Explore feature and checking out the top 10 posts to see what combination of hashtags they are using and if you can relate it to your content. Next, find niche hashtags. Use smaller hashtags with less search volume to target the audience looking for that content and identify potential customers.

Look at your competitors and make a list of what they're using; look at what they use regularly and start implementing those.

	CONTENT CALENDAR INSTRUCTIONS
STEP 1	Download your free Social Media Content Calendar Template, which I share at the end of this book.
STEP 2	*Optional* Rename the file so you can easily find it. For example '[Brand name] Content Calendar 2024.'
STEP 3	Follow the text prompts on each spreadsheet and begin building your calendar.

Check hashtag volume. If a hashtag is being used in the millions, chances are your post will be drowned out. For a safe middle ground aim to use hashtags between 10k-200k posts.

You'll need to continue to refer back to your monthly analytics (discussed below) to truly identify what is working and what is not. Note that hashtags are always changing and are NOT the key to success, but can be an effective way to get more exposure.

Finally, every social media manager should have the following documents on file to refer to every month when creating the calendar or planning out social campaigns:

- List of hashtags related to your niche.
- List of influencers & loyal followers that you can tap into for campaign launches.
- List of influencers + followers to tag and engage with in posts.

After You Post

Social media management manifests in two main ways:

1. Handling incoming messages and mentions (reactive engagement).
2. Identifying chances to establish new connections (proactive engagement).

We talked about this in Chapter 7. After you post is the perfect time to engage in proactive outreach because you're account is active.

What Social Media Managers Are Always Thinking About

Growing your social media account and getting more followers

Generally, there are four main avenues for growth: proactive engagement, hosting giveaways, boosting posts with a paid budget, and the elusive possibility of going viral.

Building a community

Building a community on social media is essential for fostering loyalty, boosting word-of-mouth referrals, and maintaining ongoing customer engagement. When you cultivate a community, you create a supportive space where clients feel valued and connected to your brand. This can be achieved by actively interacting with your followers, encouraging conversations, and sharing content that reflects their interests and needs.

TIP: Resist the urge to buy followers. In most cases, purchased followers equate to buying fake bots, which hurts your credibility with real followers. Followers who have no desire to purchase from you or engage with your content are completely worthless.

Going viral

Though there's no guaranteed formula for achieving viral status, several tactics can enhance the likelihood.

First, it's important to stay abreast of social media trends and participate when relevant to your brand. This can and will amplify visibility, but it should never be your only tactic. You will burn out quickly. Plus it's more important to be a trend setter instead of a trend follower.

Second, it's crucial to prioritize high-quality content that either narrates a compelling story or provides value through education or entertainment. Using this kind of content regularly will build you a loyal audience and also increase the likelihood that one or more of your videos will gain traction. The key is to post the same style and quality of content consistently.

Finally, create a list of ten top-performing social media videos within your community and dedicate time to recreate them. Put your own unique spin on these recreations to ensure they resonate authentically with your brand. Using existing videos as a baseline takes the guesswork out of what people are resonating with — if the video went viral, it's because it has generated watchtime and engagement. This may not work the first time you try it, but by the tenth time you should have a winner.

How to Identify What's Working (and What's Not)

Measuring your social media results removes the uncertainty from posting and simplifies the planning process. Key performance indicators (KPIs) are one way to measure success. After your first month of posting your content calendar, you need to look at growth, engagement rate, and frequency of posting then adjust your strategy based on your findings.

Professionally measuring the success of social media posts involves several key metrics. At Soar Media Group we focus on tracking:

- **Monthly follower growth.** Follower growth indicates awareness growth which is a sign of success.
- **The best and worst performing posts.** This helps us understand what resonates with our audience.
- **Best posting times.** Determining the optimal posting times helps maximize reach.
- **Engagement rate.** The engagement rate informs adjustments to content pillars based on audience interests. The industry standard engagement rate varies so I suggest googling the engagement rate that is considered average for your industry and then measuring against that.
- **Content saves.** Monitoring content saves help us understand what our audiences finds the most valuable.
- **Demographics such as location, gender, and age.** We want to know if we are actually hitting the audience we want to. Engagement is great but only when it's from your target audience. Random comments won't get you a return on investment (ROI).

After every month you need to ask yourself these questions:

- Did my account grow?
- Did my content get industry average engagement?
- Did I get direct messages (DMs) or leads?

- Are more people posting with my product?
- Are influencers and/or media outlets starting to notice me?

The best practices on the following page are what we follow at Soar Media Group. They're a quick one-page guide that all Social Media Managers should be following. Whether you're managing your brand's social media accounts on your own, or have a dedicated person, it's important that these are followed.

Social Media Checklist

On a daily basis, your brand should…

- O Reply to all direct messages and comments. This helps to grow and build a loyal following.
- O Engage in proactive outreach. Search for new community members in your relevant niche and leave them a comment or even a follow. This will also help your brand grow and be a part of a community.
- O Like and follow new pages, even competitors. Finding new pages to follow will help you further build your online community and stay up to date with key players in the social media space.

On a weekly basis, your brand should…

- O Monitor hashtags and keywords. This helps you identify what is trending and how to create content that is on par with the current landscape.
- O Interact with key users and partners. Find those dedicated fans of your brand, and make a point to interact with them so they feel loved.
- O Revisit your monthly goals to ensure you're

still on track. Goal setting on social media is important, as it helps guide your every move. Check on digital ads. View their stats, and see how they're performing.

- O Check on competitors. Reviewing your competitive landscape will keep you updated on how they are marketing their products and responding to pop culture trends.

On a monthly basis, your brand should…

- O Audit existing channels. Pull your analytic reports and review your content strategy. Check out your follower count, and see what content is doing well.
- O Refer back to your social media strategy and be honest with yourself. What's working, or rather, what's not working?
- O Try new campaigns. Maybe you really love a video technique another brand used, or just want to try something new.
- O Create your monthly social media calendar and schedule all content in one sitting. The only time you should be manually posting is if you don't have the ability to schedule the content within your calendar. In this case, timeblock when you need to post next.

Chapter Summary

- Common Mistakes Social Media Managers Make:
  - Lack of clear strategy
  - Ignoring audience engagement
  - Overlooking analytics
  - Inconsistent posting
  - Posting ads as content
  - Not staying updated with platform changes
  - Lack of authenticity
  - Focusing on quantity over quality
- Create your content calendar a month in advance to save you time.
- You can use expert tricks like scheduling posts at optimal times and using keywords in captions to increase engagement and growth.
- Adhere to the 80/20 rule (80% value, 20% promotional content).
- Experiment with relevant keywords and phrases.
- What you do on a daily, weekly, and monthly basis matters. You need to show up.
- Track KPIs like follower growth, engagement rate, best/worst performing posts, etc. monthly and adjust your strategy accordingly.

Take Action

Use our social media checklist to start assessing your social media efforts. What's working and what's not? Once you identify what's working, include this in your next content calendar.

CHAPTER 12

Optimizing Your Social Media Profile & Growing Your Account

Have you ever landed on someone's profile page on Instagram and hit follow before you even thought about it? Maybe it was someone who loves to organize. Or a brand that makes you feel like you're a part of their grassroots story. Or maybe it was a hairstylist who matches your aesthetic.

If you hit follow, it's because they made a great first impression with their account. You didn't have to think about it, because you knew, just by glancing, that you wanted to stay in the loop with that particular person or brand.

This is what a good social media account does. It sells you before you realize you've been sold to.

In this chapter you'll learn how to turn your social media profile into something people want to follow. From crafting a compelling bio to leveraging analytics for optimization, each step is designed to maximize your profile's impact and ultimately boost your business's bottom line. Whether you're starting fresh or refining an existing profile, these insights will guide you.

Update Your Profile

Your profile is often the first impression visitors get of your brand. Ensuring that your profile is complete and clear helps establish credibility and provides essential information at a glance. Your profile should include:

- **Profile Picture:** Use a high-quality image, such as a logo for businesses or a professional headshot for personal brands.
- **Bio:** Craft a concise, engaging bio that highlights who you are and what you do. What makes your brand different? Why should someone hire you? This is your chance to get a potential customer's attention so include your unique value proposition. Also include relevant keywords to enhance discoverability.
- **Contact Information:** Make it easy for followers to reach you by including your email, phone number, or other contact methods.
- **Website Link:** Direct followers to your website or a specific landing page. Update this link regularly to align with current campaigns or promotions.

Include Keywords

Incorporate relevant keywords in your bio, headline, and posts to improve discoverability through search functions and algorithms. Keywords help your profile appear in search results when users are looking for specific topics, products, or services. This increases the chances of attracting new followers who are interested in what you offer.

Conduct Regular Maintenance Checks

In early 2024, I worked with a keynote speaker eager to boost bookings through Instagram. Upon diving into her account, I found her LinkTree packed with over 20 links, creating a confusing overload. Even worse, the critical "Book Now" button led straight to a frustrating 404 Error page. This experience vividly underscored the necessity of keeping links active and streamlined. Ensuring smooth navigation not only enhances user experience but also maximizes the chances of converting visitors into clients.

Social media account maintenance is crucial for optimization. Regularly check that all links are active and lead to the correct destination, such as your website, landing page, or booking page. Ensure your profile is updated with current information, promotions, and relevant trends to maintain relevance and appeal to your audience.

Leverage Features That Can Tell Your Brand Story

Features like Instagram Highlights and 'pinned' posts are effective tools for storytelling and reinforcing your brand message. Use Instagram Highlights to educate your audience about new products or services, and pin posts that showcase your brand's journey or core values. This ensures important content remains visible and accessible to visitors, helping to establish a strong brand identity.

Be Visually Consistent

Consistent visuals across platforms are key to building strong brand recognition. This means using the same colours, fonts, and style in all your posts to create a cohesive look. Visual consistency not only makes your brand easily recognizable but also helps convey a professional and reliable image to your audience.

Include Direct Purchase Options

Streamline the purchasing process by incorporating shopping features or direct links to your website's product pages from your profile.

Simplifying the path to purchase reduces friction and enhances user experience, making it more likely for followers to complete transactions without leaving the platform.

Highlight Your Products and Services

Showing your products or services prominently on your social media profile is essential for attracting potential customers and driving sales. Use high-quality images, videos, or carousel posts to effectively demonstrate the features, benefits, and use cases of what you offer.

By highlighting specific features and benefits, you can effectively persuade followers to take the next step towards making a purchase. Clear and informative content reduces uncertainty and helps potential customers visualize how your products or services can enhance their lives.

When highlighting your products and services, it's also important to include high-quality visuals that grab attention and make a strong first impression. These kinds of visuals (images or videos) convey professionalism and quality, which are crucial in persuading followers to explore your products or services further.

Growing Your Social Media Presence

Growing your social media following requires a strategic approach that combines organic methods with paid strategies and collaboration opportunities. To increase followers organically, focus on creating valuable and engaging content that resonates with your target audience.

Consistency is key — post regularly and at optimal times to maximize visibility.

Use relevant hashtags to reach a wider audience and encourage shares and interactions.

Engage with your followers by responding to comments, messages, and mentions promptly. Building genuine relationships with your audience can lead to organic growth through word-of-mouth recommendations.

Organic Growth Tactics

Collaborating with other accounts can boost your social media following by tapping into their existing audience. Look for influencers, complementary brands, or industry partners with similar target audiences and values. Collaborate on co-branded content, giveaways, or shout-outs to cross-promote each other's profiles and reach new followers. Engaging in collaborations can provide additional exposure and credibility while fostering mutually beneficial relationships within your industry. Be selective and strategic in your partnerships to ensure alignment and maximize the impact on your follower growth strategy.

Our most-loved growth tactics at Soar Media Group are:

- Giveaways
- Partner brand giveaways
- Gifted collaborations
- Replicating viral reels in moderation

Paid Growth Tactics

In addition to organic methods, leveraging paid strategies can accelerate your follower growth. Consider running targeted ad campaigns on social media platforms to reach specific demographics and increase visibility. Use audience targeting options to hone in on potential followers who align with your ideal customer profile. Experiment with different ad formats such as carousel ads, video ads, or influencer partnerships to diversify your approach and maximize results. Set clear objectives and monitor campaign performance to optimize your investment and achieve desired outcomes.

Chapter Summary

- Ensure your profile is complete with a high-quality picture, engaging bio, contact information, and an updated website link to establish credibility and provide essential information.v
- Regularly verify that all links are active and relevant, keeping your profile updated with current information to maintain relevance and enhance user experience.
- Use features like Instagram Highlights and pinned posts to reinforce your brand message and keep important content visible, establishing a strong brand identity.
- Showcase your offerings with high-quality visuals and clear, informative content to attract potential customers and persuade them to make a purchase.

Take Action

Check in on your profile page. Is there a clear description of what you or your business offers? If someone new lands on your page, will they immediately know what you're all about? Will they hit follow or will they skip? Think like a user, not a social media manager. If you wouldn't follow or don't think the profile is strong enough to capture attention, change it.

CHAPTER 13

The Four Stages of a Social Media Sales Funnel

When I was first building up my own business, I spent my nights listening to audiobooks and podcasts from other entrepreneurs. Though much of the advice was the same, there was one tidbit that stuck with me: it's not that people don't want to buy your product. It's that they don't know you exist.

The fact is, if you have a desirable product or sevice, you can make sales. But sales won't come if noone knows you're out there.

That's why awareness (the first stage of a sales funnel) is so important.

Creating a sales funnel on social media involves strategically guiding potential customers through a series of stages aimed at converting them into paying customers. It typically includes several stages. Some sales funnels involve five or more stages, and some only four stages. I like to keep all of the sales funnels we create to four stages for ease.

It's important to note that outlining your sales funnel is one of the most overlooked aspects of managing a social media account, and usually indicates a lack of experience or understanding of using social media as a marketing tool.

If you don't have a clear funnel, you won't get sales.

This is why it's imperative that you spend time on this stage.

The customer journey always starts with awareness, then moves to consideration, then to purchase, and lastly to repeat customers. The key is to deliver valuable content at each stage of the funnel.

For example, you wouldn't message someone who just hired you to take family photos with "Did you know I take family photos?" Instead you would ask them to leave a review, or follow up with them during the holidays to let them know about your Christmas Family Photo bundle.

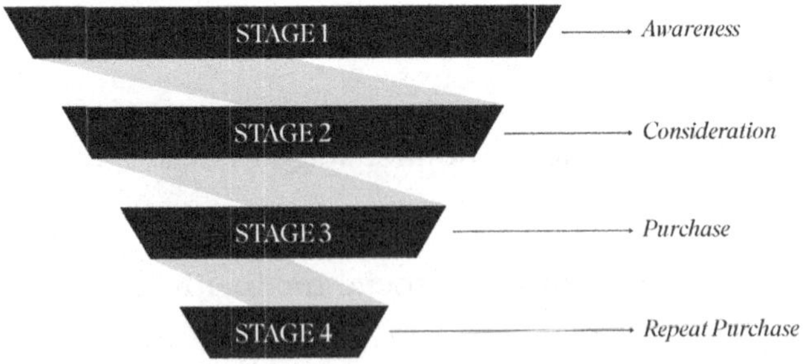

The Four Stages of a Sales Funnel

Stage 1: Awareness

My favourite way to generate awareness is through content marketing. Content marketing is a powerful tool for brands to capture attention and connect with their audience on social media.

Look at Gisou, for instance. They excel at creating content that truly resonates with their customers. Instead of solely showcasing products, Gisou shares captivating stories about the brand's heritage, their commitment to sustainability, and the journey of their natural honey-infused haircare products. You might come across videos depicting the beekeeping process or tips on maintaining healthy hair naturally. Through these efforts, Gisou builds a community of individuals who appreciate nature-inspired beauty solutions.

These types of content aren't just advertisements; they're narratives that people genuinely enjoy watching and sharing. When someone views a Gisou video about their brand values and products, they establish a deeper connection with the brand. It's about fostering relationships and offering meaningful content rather than pushing sales. This approach allows Gisou to differentiate itself in the beauty industry on social media.

The first stage of social media marketing is focused on building brand awareness and capturing the attention of your target audience.

This phase involves:

- Creating engaging and shareable content that introduces your brand.
- Using social media advertising to reach specific demographics, interests, and behaviours that align with your ideal customer profile.
- Introducing people to your brand story.
- Collaborating with influencers and industry leaders to amplify reach and credibility among relevant audiences.
- Engaging with your community by encouraging likes, shares, and comments to increase visibility and virality of content.
- Hosting giveaways where users need to tag their friends.

Stage 2: Consideration

In the consideration stage, the focus shifts towards nurturing leads and guiding them towards making a purchasing decision. This phase involves:

- Providing valuable information, product demonstrations, comparisons to why you're better than the competition, and testimonials to address customer questions and objections.
- Creating exclusive promotions or discounts.
- Offering free trials or demonstrations.
- Retargeting ads to re-engage users who have shown interest in your brand or products.

- Showing social proof through positive reviews and testimonials to build trust and credibility.

Stage 3: Purchase

The purchase stage is where prospective customers transition into paying customers. Converting leads into customers is a critical milestone that demonstrates the effectiveness of social media marketing efforts and generates revenue. This phase involves:

- Implementing a clear and compelling Call To Action (CTA) to guide users towards making a purchase (e.g., "Shop Now," "Book Now," "Contact Me For A Free Consult").
- Ensuring a user-friendly checkout or booking process to minimize friction and purchase abandonment.
- Offering limited-time promotions, discounts, or incentives to incentivize immediate purchase decisions.
- Providing responsive and helpful customer support to address pre-purchase inquiries and concerns.

Stage 4: Repeat Purchase and Loyalty

The final stage focuses on fostering customer loyalty and encouraging repeat purchases, turning one-time buyers into brand advocates. Cultivating customer loyalty is essential for maximizing customer lifetime value, reducing churn, and generating ongoing revenue through repeat purchases and referrals. Repeat customers are also the most profitable since they already know and trust you. This phase involves:

- Sending thank you emails and post-purchase communications to show appreciation and offer additional support.
- Gathering feedback to identify areas for improvement and demonstrate a commitment to customer satisfaction.
- Implementing loyalty programs or rewards programs to incentivize repeat purchases and foster long-term relationships.
- Encouraging customers to share their experiences through User-Generated Content (UGC), showcasing brand loyalty and authenticity.
- Providing exceptional customer service to address any issues or inquiries promptly.
- Upselling and cross-selling: recommend complementary products or upgrades based on customer preferences and behaviour.

Engagement and Relationship Building

Encouraging engagement with your community is crucial for turning your social media presence into a profitable venture. Responding promptly to comments, messages, and mentions shows your audience that you value their input and are attentive to their needs. Actively interacting with your followers helps to foster relationships and build a loyal community, which is key to driving repeat business.

Engagement also boosts your visibility on social media platforms, as algorithms favour profiles with high interaction rates. The more you engage with your audience, the more likely your posts are to be seen by a broader audience, increasing your reach and potential customer base.

Furthermore, engaged customers are more likely to share their positive experiences with your brand, providing you with valuable word-of-mouth marketing. This can lead to new customers discovering your products through trusted recommendations from their peers.

Social media is not just about broadcasting messages, it's about forging genuine connections that resonate with your audience. One of the best ways to do this is through authentic interactions.

Take the time to respond to comments, ask questions, and show appreciation for your followers. By nurturing these relationships, you're not only building trust but also cultivating a community around your brand.

When it comes to engaging with followers, consistency is key. Show up regularly with valuable content that speaks directly to their interests and needs. Encourage conversations by posing thoughtful questions and sparking discussions. Be present and responsive, treating each interaction as an opportunity to deepen connections.

TIP: Repeat customers are the most profitable since they already trust and know your brand. Nurturing these relationships through consistent engagement can lead to higher lifetime value and increased sales. For example, thanking a loyal customer for their continued support with a personalized message or exclusive discount can reinforce their loyalty and encourage further purchases.

Additionally, don't shy away from addressing feedback or concerns openly and constructively. This transparency not only strengthens trust but also showcases your commitment to listening and improving based on customer input.

Every interaction is a chance to build meaningful relationships that drive business growth. Keep nurturing these relationships, and they will fuel your business growth.

How to Create Loyal Brand Supporters

Retaining customers and fostering loyalty is essential for the long-term success of your business. Building strong relationships with your customers starts with providing exceptional products or services and ensuring a positive customer experience. Focus on delivering value and addressing customer needs to keep them coming back. Personalize your interactions by addressing customers by name and offering tailored recommendations or exclusive offers based on their preferences.

Leveraging social proof is another effective way to drive referrals and advocacy. Display customer reviews, ratings, and endorsements prominently to demonstrate the value of your offerings. Incorporate social share buttons and referral programs to incentivize existing customers to refer friends and family. By leveraging social proof, you can amplify positive word-of-mouth and attract new customers through trusted recommendations from your existing customer base.

Ultimately, optimizing for retention and advocacy requires a customer-centric approach. Listen to customer feedback, address concerns promptly, and continuously seek opportunities to exceed expectations. Building strong relationships with your customers will not only drive repeat business but also turn satisfied customers into brand advocates who promote your business to others. By focusing on providing value, fostering engagement, and leveraging social proof, you can create a loyal customer base that drives sustained growth and success for your business.

Optimizing Your Sales Funnel by Measuring Performance

To make the most of your data, focus on actionable takeaways. Identify trends and patterns that can inform strategic adjustments. Experiment with different content formats, audience targeting strategies, or ad placements based on performance insights. Embrace a growth mindset, viewing each metric as a stepping stone toward refining your approach and achieving your goals.

Remember, measuring performance isn't just about analysis — it's about empowerment. By regularly reviewing your social media performance, you gain the clarity and confidence needed to bring in more sales.

TIP: Offer exclusive promotions throughout the year. Announce exclusive discounts, sales events, or limited-time offers on your social media profile to incentivize purchases and reward customer loyalty. Creating a sense of urgency encourages immediate action from followers and increases conversion rates, as followers are motivated to take advantage of special deals before they expire.

Chapter Summary

- Without a clear funnel, achieving sales becomes challenging.
- Each stage of the social media marketing journey, from awareness to loyalty, plays a crucial role in nurturing long-term customer relationships.
- The journey typically begins with awareness, moves through consideration and purchase, and culminates in repeat customers.
- Optimize your sales funnel requires a customer-centric approach, focusing on delivering value, fostering engagement, and leveraging social proof to create a loyal customer base that drives sustained growth.

CHAPTER 14
Tools That Killer Social Media Managers Use

Navigating the ever-evolving landscape of social media platforms and strategies can be overwhelming without the right tools at your disposal. In this chapter, we'll explore a curated selection of social media tools that we use at Soar Media Group, ranging from free to low-cost options, each offering unique features and benefits to streamline your social media management efforts.

Whether you're a seasoned marketer or just starting out, these tools are essential for optimizing your presence across various platforms and maximizing your impact in the digital sphere.

Iconosquare

Iconosquare is an analytics platform that connects to Facebook, Instagram, and TikTok. The platform provides detailed analytics to help you measure growth and engagement, as well as monitor competitors. They have a scheduling tool, though my team and I only use the program for analytics purposes. I find that the analytics are much more detailed than the native analytics within Instagram, Facebook and TikTok and provide a great overview of what is working and what is not.

The growth tool also allows us to effectively measure curves in growth — we see jumps when we host giveaways or a big influencer campaign. I also love using this tool to measure growth because we're able to set custom date ranges which helps us show clients a more comprehensive overview of our success. For example, below I've set the dates for our @soarmediagroupinc Instagram account from January to April. We can see a clear growth upwards.

There are various paid tiers for Iconosquare pending how many users you will have and how many accounts you will link. Overall, the basic tier provides informative analytics that can be used to guide your social media marketing.

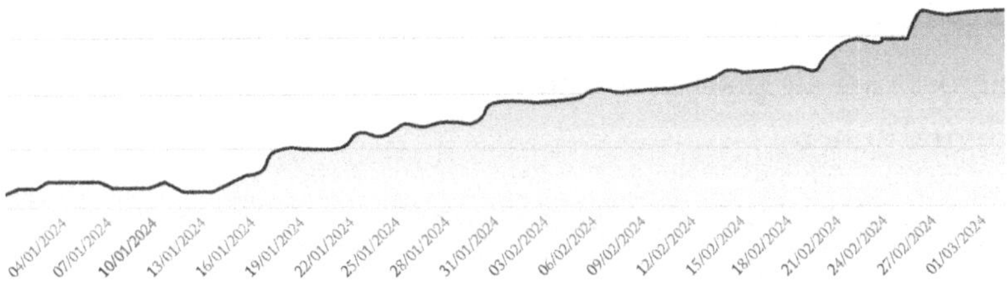

META Business Suite

META Business Suite is an essential tool for social media managers, particularly for scheduling content on Instagram and Facebook. This tool allows you to manage comments and inquiries from both Instagram and Facebook in one spot. You can mark conversations as 'done' or you can flag them to remind yourself to return to them.

Although META Business Suite is a must for social media managers, I will warn you that the native analytics have gone downhill. There aren't a lot of valuable metrics within the platform, which is why a tool like Iconosquare is useful.

Remember, in order to be a ***killer*** social media manager, you need robust insights and analytics to track performance metrics and optimize social media strategies.

Moreover, for advertising purposes, having a Business Suite account is crucial. While some clients may prefer using their personal ad accounts, it can pose significant challenges as businesses scale and require more comprehensive campaign management. Business Suite allows for better organization, collaboration, and scalability, ensuring smoother operations and more effective advertising campaigns in the long run.

META Business Suite is a free tool to use, and is a non-negotiable tool for the social media managers on our team. If you are managing a Facebook page and Instagram account at the same time, you need to know how to use META Business Suite.

Canva

Canva is a graphic design platform that helps users create high-quality designs with little effort. It's user-friendly with a vast library of templates, fonts, images, and design elements. Virtually every novice and seasoned social media manager uses this platform.

If you have Canva Pro, be sure to use the 'brand tool kit' tool to insert your branded fonts and colours so that everything you create is consistent.

Spend time combing through Canva to find a variety of designs you like. Then use platforms like Pinterest to see what speaks to you. Cross-reference your favourite designs with your brand, and if they feel like they fit, start to edit them with the message you want to get across. Maybe you want to make an inspirational quote, or share a review (customer testimonial), or dive deep into the ingredients used in your product.

Mastering Canva will take practice but it will be worth it. I also suggest paying for the premium version of Canva. The premium version gives you access to better design templates, team sharing, and stock photos and graphics that you can use as part of your subscription.

Adobe Products: Photoshop, Premiere Pro

Adobe products like Photoshop and Premiere Pro are most often used by agencies or individual photographers and videographers for content creation and editing. These tools offer advanced features and capabilities that enable professionals to produce high-quality visual and video content tailored to their brand's needs.

With Photoshop, you can design eye-catching graphics, edit images, and create visually engaging posts. Premiere Pro, on the other hand, allows for seamless video editing, enabling managers to craft polished and professional videos for social media platforms.

These are tools that require experience and skill. That said, if you are able to master them, you won't regret it. The editing capabilities for YouTube videos, Reels, and TikToks are unmatched. Adobe products are paid for monthly or yearly. Prices range based on which program you're using.

CapCut

CapCut is a user-friendly video editing tool that many social media managers who don't know how to use Premiere Pro use instead. Actually, many of our professional editors will sometimes use CapCut instead of Premiere Pro. This is because the platform offers a variety of TikTok friendly fonts and templates that are not available on Premiere Pro.

With features like trimming, cutting, merging, adding filters, and special effects, CapCut enables managers to produce high-quality video content without the need for extensive technical expertise. The built-in templates are often used for viral trends like the Kid Cudi Day 'N' Night sunglasses trend (which, yes, I created for my wedding content).

Why would someone use CapCut instead of editing directly in TikTok or Instagram?

There is no right answer to this, it's just about preference. My team edits on virtually every editing platform out there. We will edit in CapCut if there is a viral template we are using, or we will edit in Premiere Pro if we need precision editing (to the millisecond), or we might edit in Instagram or TikTok if the video is a simple compilation.

Social media managers often choose to edit in CapCut because it provides more precision editing than editing in-app. For example, it's difficult to cut to the music in-app so you might choose to use CapCut.

CapCut should be reserved for social media videos only. If you are looking for a high-quality brand video that is used for your website or distributed to retailers, I suggest investing into a seasoned video team.

CapCut is available for both mobile and desktop.

There is a free version of CapCut, but to access all of the trending templates you'll need the paid version. My advice? Upgrade to the paid version. It's worth it.

Google Keyword Planner

Google Keyword Planner, I like to think, is my secret weapon when it comes to content strategy and concepts. The tool helps social media managers identify high-value keywords related to their industry or niche. By incorporating these keywords into social media posts, managers can improve the discoverability of their content on search engines, ultimately driving more traffic to their website or social media profiles.

In fact, my personal blog post about Hermes Sandals was only created because I first found that the keyword phrase 'are the Hermes Sandals worth it' had a very high search volume on Google. I created a blog post with high-quality images and then distributed those images onto Pinterest. For the past year I've received over 14,000 Pinterest views per month because of that post, and my images related to the blog post have been pinned hundreds of times. The blog post and subsequent social media content was strategically planned based on the information I gathered from Google Keyword Planner.

SEO on social media is often overlooked, but it can have a significant impact on discoverability. With platforms like Instagram, Pinterest, and YouTube evolving into search engines of their own, it's crucial to optimize content for search.

Use tools like Google Keyword Planner to identify keywords your audience is searching for and integrate these into captions and hashtags.

By analyzing keyword search volume and trends, social media managers can gain insights into topics that are popular among their target audience. This data can inform content planning and help managers create social media posts that resonate with their followers' interests and preferences.

Google Keyword Planner offers data-driven insights that can guide content topics. Plus, it's free to use!

Dropbox

Dropbox is a cloud-hosted platform designed for storing and sharing files and documents online, enabling users to access them from any internet-connected device.

Dropbox is a great tool to use to store large files such as video, images, or audio files. We use Dropbox for all of our client work. There is a free version of Dropbox, but if you are creating content consistently, you will likely need the paid version. This will help free up space on your computer, laptop, or phone while ensuring you can still access old files.

Chapter Summary

- Tools can help you make better strategic choices and create high-quality or trendy content.
- Iconosquare helps measure growth, engagement, and monitor competitors.
- Canva is a user-friendly graphic design platform with a vast library of templates, fonts, and design elements.
- Adobe offers advanced tools for image and video editing. This is better suited if you have video or photography experience. If you don't, that's okay! This tool is not essential to show up on social media.
- CapCut is a user-friendly video editing tool for social media content. This is the tool that many TikTokers use for viral templates or to create their own templates.
- META Business Suite is essential for scheduling content on Instagram and Facebook, although their native analytics are not as good as they used to be.
- Google Keyword Planner identifies high-value keywords for content strategy.
- Dropbox is a great tool to use to store files and ensure you don't run out of space on your primary device.

CHAPTER 15

Entrepreneurs Who Are Killing It on Social Media

In crafting this book, my goal was to offer insights from over a decade of experience. However, I also wanted to spotlight the remarkable journeys of fellow female entrepreneurs who are building thriving communities on social media, each forging their unique path to success.

I had the privilege of interviewing each of these entrepreneurs, delving into their stories and strategies for success. I trust that their perspectives will inspire and inform your own journeys towards social media success.

LOHN

LOHN was founded in 2018 by two Canadian women, Katerina Juskey and Victoria Mierzwa. Since launching, LOHN has grown to be one of Canada's top candle brands, with products carried in over 150 retailers across North

America and notable media coverage in *The Globe and Mail*, *Elle Canada*, and *Well + Good*.

Website: shoplohn.com

Instagram 16K followers: @lohnofficial

TikTok 1.1K followers: @lohnofficial

What advice would you offer to entrepreneurs who are just beginning to build their brand on social media?

Be the real you! Don't be afraid to show up with authenticity, whether it's through showing your face or telling your story through your brand's account. When viewers see your genuinity, that is when you really shine.

What are some of the challenges you have faced while using social media to grow your business?

The algorithm changes and updates. It feels like we get bombarded with Instagram and TikTok growth tips on a daily basis. It's so hard to keep track!

What makes your brand stand out on social media?

Our colourful elements, passion for design, and attention to detail.

What are some of the innovative ways you have used social media to engage with your customers?

This is not related to social media specifically, but we have a scent quiz which has been a really fun way to engage with our customers and have them learn which scent they'll love best from our collection.

What is something every entrepreneur should know about social media that's not spoken about often? Why do you feel this is important to know?

It's okay to take a break sometimes. Social media can be very overwhelming, and although we are obliged to use it on a daily basis, it can be really difficult to witness virtual wins and successes 24/7 while undergoing the rollercoaster ride of running a business. I delete Instagram and TikTok from my phone for days at a time every month and my mental health thanks me for it everytime!

Midnight Paloma

Midnight Paloma is a self-care beauty company that is redefining what eco-friendly beauty means. This female-founded and Canadian-made company offers vegan and cruelty free collections that are handcrafted by a small team in Vancouver, BC. In addition to receiving glowing reviews from publications like *Poosh, Who What Wear, Cosmopolitan,* and *GirlBoss*, the company has collaborated with large Canadian influencers like Jillian Harris.

Website: midnightpaloma.com

Instagram 25.8K followers: @midnightpaloma

Which social media platforms does Midnight Paloma focus on, and how did you decide on these platforms?

For social media, we've found the most success on Instagram. It's been a natural growth, from the very beginning. But we definitely try them all out. Facebook and

TikTok are included in all of our social plans, each platform has such a different customer reach.

How does Midnight Paloma measure the success of its social media efforts?

Engagement is definitely my signal for success, when I see our followers commenting, liking, and sharing our content, it feels like a big win.

Can you share any specific tactics or campaigns that have been successful in driving sales from social media?

Multi-branded giveaways and partnerships with larger influencers have been behind our larger success stories. Anything that gets a buzz going and is collab based! I've learned over the years, there are many ways to 'collaborate' — using another brand/person's platform is a great way to reach new people, and it's fun!

What advice would you give to entrepreneurs looking to leverage social media for business success, particularly in the beauty or skincare industry?

It's a tough industry to crack because there are a lot of people in space! But I think if you stay true to what you are doing, and have real authenticity, you will cultivate the customers you want following you.

Are there any specific tactics you believe are essential for achieving six-figure results through social media marketing?

If I'm being completely transparent, I haven't gotten that high yet! It's an ever-changing platform, so you have to be able to pivot and adjust to all the new updates. But 6 figures is something to work towards.

Simply Beautiful Decor

Simply Beautiful Decor is a premier event design and décor company based in Niagara-on-the-Lake, renowned for transforming ordinary spaces into extraordinary experiences. With a keen eye for detail and a passion for creativity, they specialize in elegant weddings, corporate events, and stylish celebrations. They have elevated weddings for NHL players and hundreds of couples across the GTA with their exceptional rentals, and they were the rental company I chose for my own wedding in 2023.

Website: www.simplybeautifuldecor.ca

Instagram 47.8K followers: @simplybeautifuldecor

What advice would you offer to entrepreneurs who are just beginning to build their brand on social media?

Create High-Quality Visual Content. In the wedding industry, visual appeal is crucial. I believe that investing in professional photography to showcase your brand/inventory is the starting point. Regularly update your feed, engage with your audience, and collaborate within your industry.

What are some of the challenges you have faced while using social media to grow your business?

Keeping Up with Trends. Keeping up with new social media trends and reflecting them in our social media content has been challenging. I find that it requires continuous research to remain relevant and appealing which can be very time consuming, resource-intensive, and overwhelming.

What makes your brand stand out on social media?

We work extremely hard to keep our inventory fresh and up-to-date, frequently adding and designing new inventory, like our in-house developed printed linen collection and tabletop pieces gathered from all over the world along with furniture pieces that clients cannot find at other rental companies. This commitment to variety and quality helps us lead the industry across both Canada and the USA.

We focus on building strong collaborations with event planners, photographers, and other industry professionals. These partnerships not only expand our reach but also enhance our credibility. By working with trusted names in the industry, we can tap into new audiences and add a layer of trust and authenticity to our brand.

What are some of the innovative ways you have used social media to engage with your customers?

We create and share inspiration boards and mood boards that feature our rentals in various themed settings. These boards help our followers visualize how our items can be used for various events.

We share behind-the-scenes content from our warehouse, setup processes, and product sourcing which gives our audience a glimpse into the hard work and creativity that goes into our business. I find that it builds trust and allows our followers to feel more connected to our brand.

CHAPTER 16

Your Turn to Kill It

So, you've finally climbed the social media mountain. How does it feel?

Social media is a journey. A marathon that you train for every day. I know it can get overwhelming. There's always more content, more trends, more changes, and it's easy to feel like you don't know where to start. I get it. As I write this, I'm coming back from a six-month social media break. But here's the thing: the key to getting started is simple. You just need to start.

I hope this book has given you not just the confidence to begin but a fresh perspective. You've now got the strategy, the tools, and a game plan to build your social media with purpose.

If there's one thing you should walk away with from ***Killer Socials***, it's this: You don't need millions of followers to succeed. Trust me, even a modest following — when you show up for them — can lead to real growth, brand opportunities, and lasting success.

Start small and build momentum. Every post, every story, every interaction is a chance to grow and learn. And yes, you'll fail sometimes, but that's just part of the process.

Learn from your competitors, check in on what works, but never stop experimenting or creating.

Remember that consistency and adaptability are your ride-or-die friends in this game. Building a social media presence isn't about having a perfect, buzzword-filled plan, it's about showing up every day.

Create content that has value and engage with your community like they matter. Because they do.

People follow people who are real. Whether you're giving something away for free, sharing your knowledge or just showing up as yourself, it's important to be authentic. Your audience should feel seen, heard and valued.

Don't be afraid to recycle high-performing content. It's doesn't mean you're being stale or boring. It means you understand what your audience wants to see.

And finally, remember to zoom out and look at the big picture. Social media success isn't about going viral overnight, it's about building a community, fostering loyalty, and driving long-term growth. Keep learning, keep adapting, and always stay true to yourself.

Your audience is out there, waiting to connect with you. So go out and ***kill*** it!

Join our social media marketing community on Instagram by visiting our profile and giving us a follow at @soarmediagroupinc.

Your Free Social Media Content Calendar Template

Stay ahead of the game with our free Social Media Content Calendar template! This invaluable tool is designed to help you plan your social media posts on a monthly basis, ensuring you stay organized and consistent with your content strategy.

Simply visit www.soarmediagroupinc.com/free-social-media-calendar-template to download your template and start streamlining your social media planning process. With this template, you'll be able to schedule posts, track key dates, and maintain a cohesive online presence effortlessly.

Notes & References

Letter from the Author

1. Johnson, Kristin. "Why Social Media vs. Traditional Media is not the Debate You Should Care About." Sprout Social, 18 May 2021, https://sproutsocial.com/insights/social-media-vs-traditional-media/

Chapter 2: Social Media's Allure & Managerial Pitfalls

1. Aldrich, Anna Zarra. "Finding Social Support Through Social Media During COVID Lockdowns." University of Connecticut, 24 June 24 2022, https://today.uconn.edu/2022/06/finding-social-support-through-social-media-during-covid-lockdowns/
2. Shearer, Elisa and Mitchell, Amy. "News Use Across Social Media Platforms 2020." pewresearch.org, 12 January 2021, https://www.pewresearch.org/journalism/2021/01/12/news-use-across-social-media-platforms-in-2020/
3. Mohsin, Maryam. "10 Social Media Statistics You Need To Know In 2024 [Infographic]." Oberlo, 13 October 2023, https://www.oberlo.com/blog/social-media-marketing-statistics
4. Sprout Social. "New Research Reveals Influencers Significantly Drive Purchasing Decisions." 25 April 2024, https://sproutsocial.com/insights/press/new-research-reveals-influencers-significantly-drive-purchasing-decisions/

Chapter 3: Picking the Right Social Media Platform

1. Newberry, Christina. "36 Must-Know Instagram Stats for Marketers in 2024." HootSuite, 23 July 2024 https://blog.hootsuite com/instagram-statistics/
2. Influencer Marketing Hub. "44 Vital TikTok Stats to Inform Your Marketing Strategy." Influencer Marketing Hub, 13 September 2024, https://influencermarketinghub.com/tiktok-stats/
3. Kozlowska, Hanna. "US Facebook users are getting older." Quartz, 11 September 2019, https://qz.com/1707287/use-of-facebook-among- senior-americans-has-doubled-over-recent-years
4. Newberry, Christina. "36 X (Twitter) Stats That Matter to Marketers in 2024." HootSuite, 3 April 2024, https://blog.hootsuite.com/twitter-statistics/
5. McLachlan, Stacey. "19 X (Twitter) Demographics for Marketers in 2024." HootSuite, 7 May 2024, https://blog.hootsuite.com/twitter-demographics/
6. Habig, Jim. "Pinterest Presents: a new vision for the future." Pinterest Business, 3 March 2021, https://business.pinterest.com/en-ca/blog/pinterest-presents-a-new-vision-for-the-future/
7. Dixon, Stacy Jo. "Percentage of U.S. adults who use Pinterest as of February 2021, by age group." Statista, 1 August 2022, https://www.statista.com/statistics/246183/share-of-us-internet-users-who-

use-pinterest-by-age-group/business.pinterest.com,https://business.pinterest.com/en-ca/shopping/

8. Moeller, Susan. "Are You Making the Most of the BIGGEST Seasons on Pinterest?" Tailwind, 31 October 2019, https://www.tailwindapp.com/blog/are-you-making-the-most-of-the-biggest-seasons-on-pinterest
9. Aslam, Salman. "YouTube by the Numbers: Stats, Demographics & Fun Facts." Omnicore, 10 January 2024, https://www.omnicoreagency.com/youtube-statistics/
10. Macready, Hannah. "27 Inspiring YouTube Stats to Know in 2024." Hootsuite, 4 April 2024, https://blog.hootsuite.com/youtube-stats-marketers/
11. Aslam, Salman. "90 LinkedIn Statistics You Need to Know in 2024." Omnicore, 11 January 2024, https://www.omnicoreagency.com/linkedin-statistics/
12. Martin, Michelle. "2024 LinkedIn Demographics That Matter to Marketers." Hootsuite, 21 February 2024, https://blog.hootsuite.com/linkedin-demographics-for-business/

Chapter 6: I. Invest in Content Marketing

1. Andreacchi, Maria-Teresa [@mariateresa_andreacchi]. "I think They Did Pretty Well." Instagram. 18 Oct. 2023, https://www.instagram.com/reel/CyjaJk-ucyp/
2. Andreacchi, Maria-Teresa [@mariateresa_andreacchi].

"Hits and Misses at my Wedding." Instagram. 6 Nov. 2023, https://www.instagram.com/reel/CzUrpgELprI/

3. Andreacchi, Maria-Teresa [@mariateresa_andreacchi]. "Well, Something Had to go Wrong, right?!," Instagram. 9 Nov. 2023, https://www.instagram.com/reel/Czb_ZWYOYw5/
4. Aliaj, Orenca. "Social media influencers named as stock market listing risk factor." Financial Times, 11 January 2020, https://www.ft.com/content/0dacea5c-3402-11ea-9703-eea0cae3f0de

Chapter 7: Listen to Your Audience

1. Demeku, Amanda. "Instagram Hashtags: Everything You Need To Know in 2024." Later Blog, 23 May 2024, https://later.com/blog/ultimate-guide-to-using-instagram-hashtags/

Chapter 9: E. Engage Before You Sell

1. Nosto. "The Consumer Content Report: Influence in the Digital Age." 2019, https://www.nosto.com/blog/consumer-content-report-influence-in-the-digital-age-2/
2. Sprout Social. "Sprout Social Index Edition XVII: Accelerate." 2022, https://media.sproutsocial.com/uploads/Sprout-Social-Index-Edition-XVII-Accelerate.pdf

3. Edelman. "2021 Trust Barometer Special Report: The Belief-Driven Employee." 2021, https://www.edelman.com/trust/2021-trust-barometer/belief-driven-employee

ABOUT THE AUTHOR

Maria-Teresa Andreacchi is the founder and Chief Creative Strategist of Soar Media Group Inc., a social media marketing agency located in Toronto. For over a decade she has been sharing her expertise with Canada's signature brands such as Meridian Credit Union, Motusbank, Joyburst, No Sugar Company, and Children's Mental Health Ontario, to name a few. Most recently, her team has worked with artists like Vanilla Ice and The D.O.C.

Before creating Soar Media Group, Maria-Teresa worked in the corporate and agency world, specialising in social media marketing and public relations. She was one of the first in Toronto to create a lifestyle blog, and is considered a digital pioneer in her field — at 24 years-old she was training the CEO of Meridian Credit Union how to use Twitter and was part of the two-man team behind bringing Canada's largest credit union to one of the top 100 credit unions in the world using social media.

Her company produces, manages and executes a wide variety of digital content such as social media content, digital commercials, brand photoshoots, influencer campaigns, and website content.

In 2020, her team created, produced and executed Ontario Caregiver Organization's podcast Time to Talk, a five-star rated podcast that is hosted by Toronto media personality Michelle Jobin. In 2022, her team initiated the #Joywalk Instagram campaign for Joyburst which partnered with Canadian CFL players and non-traditional creators to compliment the national Super Bowl LVI commercial. The digital campaign was seen by over 200,000 users and did so primarily using micro-creators. Her and her team also digitally launched No Sugar Company and Joyburst from scratch — both Canada's fastest growing brands.

She is a fearless leader and a dedicated mentor, always ready to share her knowledge and experience.

Maria-Teresa's work has been featured in publications across Canada such as the award-winning *Vacations* magazine, and *Huffington Post Canada*, while her launch of Soar Media Group was seen in *Toronto Life*.

To contact Maria-Teresa directly, connect with her on Instagram at @mariateresa_andreacchi.

MARIA-TERESA ANDREACCHI

Made in the USA
Monee, IL
08 November 2026

67380491R00111